THE BIBLE
IN 20th CENTURY
ART

Introduced by
Nicholas Usherwood

PAGODA

The Bible text in this publication is from
the Good News Bible (Today's English
Version), published by The Bible Societies
and Collins. Old Testament: © American
Bible Society 1976. Deuterocanonicals:
© American Bible Society 1979.
New Testament: © American Bible
Society 1966, 1971, 1976.
Used by permission.

ISBN 0 946326 34 7

Typeset in Sabon by DP Press, Sevenoaks, Kent
Originated, printed, and bound by Sagdos in Italy

Cover: *Third Allegory*
Ben Shahn
The Vatican Museum of Modern Religious Art;
photo Scala

CONTENTS

Foreword   4

Introduction   5

The Plates   9

The Artists   91

ANNIGONI	MAGRITTE
BACON	MODERSOHN-BECKER
BECKMANN	NASH
BOMBERG	NEWMAN
BUFFET	NOLDE
BURRA	PICASSO
CHAGALL	REDON
DE CHIRICO	ROHLFS
CORINTH	ROMAIN
DALI	ROUAULT
DENIS	SHALOM OF SAFED
ENSOR	SCHMIDT-ROTTLUFF
FUCHS	SHAHN
GLEIZES	SIQUEIROS
GROSZ	SMITS
KLIMT	SPENCER
KOENIG	SUTHERLAND
KOKOSCHKA	SZUBERT
KRAMER	VEĆENAJ
LEVINE	WEIGHT

Glossary   110

Acknowledgements   111

FOREWORD

To a large degree, art inspired by biblical themes is most widely associated with centuries passed and not with this era. Yet many great contemporary masters have in fact produced and continue to produce works of a fervently religious nature; while others (perhaps surprisingly, agnostics and atheists among them) have also often opted to visualize a biblical heritage. Our book thus sets out to quell the myth that neither Old nor New Testament themes find much of a place today in painting.

It has been both a delightful and somewhat difficult task to select the works reproduced. Some of them are personal favourites of our authors: others have been chosen to illustrate variety in style and approach. The collection will, we trust, not only inform but inspire.

S.P.

THE AUTHORS

NICHOLAS USHERWOOD is a foremost British art critic and historian, who regularly makes contributions to several art magazines, such as *Art and Artists, The Antique Collector* and *Country Life*, as well as major exhibition catalogues. He has worked at both the Royal Academy in London, and as Deputy Director of Exhibitions at the British Museum.

PAUL HOLBERTON has worked on many books as both art historian and editor, notably including Sir David Piper's four-volume Encyclopaedia of Art. He has also written articles for various guide books and magazines, including *The Burlington Magazine, Word and Image* and *The Journal of the Warburg and Courtauld Institutes*. Whilst also writing a book on architecture, he is completing a doctorate with the Warburg Institute, London, on Renaissance art in Venice.

INTRODUCTION

In a century commonly characterized as anti-religious and ardently materialist, a century in which God has been declared 'dead' many times over, a book devoted to showing the Bible in twentieth century art might on first consideration seem to have little to offer. "Is there any?" is perhaps the immediate reaction; and even the most committed and knowledgeable apologists of both twentieth century and religious art in general can be found bewailing the fact that "the twentieth century has produced so little art in the service of spirituality." Yet one of the excitements, and surprises, of putting together a book like this is the slow revelation of just how much there in fact is, and of what astonishing richness and variety.

This makes one wonder at all those books on the Bible in Art which never include a picture painted later than 1900: for here is a sequence of images as profound and as hard-won as any in the history of art, the stronger perhaps for their being won against all the odds, the better for the way they deal with their subject in ways relevant to the problems of our own century.

In saying all that, there is no attempt to claim for the twentieth century a quantity of religious art that can compare with the Romanesque or Baroque styles of art of the great ages of faith. Rather, it is to say how remarkable it is, given the fact that we live in a society which we can no longer claim to be predominantly religious in upbringing or outlook, that it is there at all, and in forms that are both spiritually and aesthetically uplifting and satisfying.

Why should this be? Mark Chagall, a Jewish artist who became in his lifetime one of the greatest interpreters of the Bible – both Old and New Testaments – put his finger on the underlying impulse with characteristic shrewdness when he remarked that: "Everything may change in our demoralized world except the heart, Man's love and his striving to know the divine. Painting, like all poetry, has a part in the divine; people feel this today just as much as they used to." As he suggests, what

in reality has happened is that the monumental physical disasters and profound spiritual and intellectual upheavals of our times have made men look for religious reassurance of one kind or another, more than ever before. This has, as a consequence, returned art once again to the task of dealing with things of the spirit. And though Judaism and Christianity have no monopoly of any belief in the divine, the Bible stories of both the Old and New Testaments still contain a profound and recognized (and recognizable) core of truths about the human condition that numerous contemporary artists have found attractive as themes.

One of the greatest challenges of Bible stories for twentieth century artists has been essentially one of interpretation, of how to express universal truths in the light of all the dramatic changes that have taken place in Man's understanding of himself over the last century. "A history of art is", as the critic G.H. Hamilton has pointed out, "a history of consciousness, and a history of modern art is uniquely a history of self-consciousness." Freud and Jung made us look uncomfortably into ourselves in a way that it was impossible to go back upon, while Rutherford's smashing of the atom shattered, as Kandinsky perceived, the comfortable material realities of everyday life once and for all. Such upheavals have, of course, been disastrous to conventional ecclesiastical ideas of Christian art, rooted as they were, and sadly still often are, in the pieties of nineteenth century materialism: and time and again, religious authorities have either rejected or ignored so many of the finest religious artists of our century.

In the reaction to Impressionism can be found the beginnings of an art more concerned with expressing those 'interior' states of mind that can be said to characterize the art of the twentieth century; and there, in the formal contemplations of Cézanne and the poetic, primitive symbolism of Gauguin are the real foundations of modern religious art.

One picture, essentially twentieth century in

character, would seem to mark the beginning of this turning of the tide, and interestingly it is based straightforwardly on a biblical theme: Gauguin's *The Vision after the Sermon* (also known as *Jacob wrestling with the Angel*), 1888 (National Gallery of Scotland, Edinburgh). In this revolutionary work, remarkably his first in the new Symbolist style it embodies and which he more or less invented, Gauguin in one leap overcomes the fundamental inability of the Impressionists to represent anything which cannot be perceived. The painting shows outward and inward events simultaneously. The priest and the peasants, and their recollection of the sermon they have just heard (on Jacob wrestling with the angel), are clearly distinguished by discrepancies of colour, scale and perspective. The unnaturalistic areas of pure colour (notably the dominant red ground of the field), the flattened forms of the faces and headdresses, creating mysterious turning rhythms, and the bold division of the painting into physical and psychical halves by the gnarled tree trunk – all show Gauguin's ability to use abstract pictorial means to achieve a mood of heightened mystical intensity, thereby employing many of the formal anti-naturalistic devices he had observed in the wayside calvaries of Brittany where it was painted. This desire to explore the powerful expressive effects of the primitive was to provide a vital impulse to much of his best religious art.

Gauguin's achievement in synthesizing the abstract rhythms of colour, line and form to express moods and emotions was, of course, also one which van Gogh was also working towards in his own particular way. Indeed, he and Gauguin had a powerful mutual effect on one another: and to Gauguin's discoveries, van Gogh added another powerful element – the vigorous, rhythmic brush strokes with which he put down the highly personal and symbolic language of colour and form on the canvas.

Van Gogh's early form of Expressionism and Gauguin's primitive, poetic Symbolism provided the gateways through which much of the most significant religious art of the twentieth century was to pass. They were, however, to find their strongest followers not in France – where, with the exception of Rouault, little great religious art developed – but rather in Germany. There, fusing with a long if erratic and highly emotional tradition of religious art, they sparked off that dynamic burst of creative energy in the early years of the century known by the general description of German Expressionism, a rather loose-knit description of a movement which covered a wide range of artists over a historical period of some forty years or more.

In the early pre-First World War period, the outstanding exponent of biblically oriented art was, of course, Emil Nolde. Both as a man and in his art, Nolde seems to epitomize so many of those qualities that have been fundamental to the production of the great religious art of our century. Deeply religious, he was also frequently racked with doubt, but this was a doubt that was to power his work. Like others, too, he found in other faiths, as well as his own, crucial sources for his finest pictures.

An interest in primitive art was perhaps also a key element for Nolde. However, it was not – as it was, say, for Picasso or Matisse, or even some of his German Expressionist colleagues – an aesthetic appreciation but rather a psychological one. The brutally simplified drawing, the broad flat patterns, the themes of ecstatic emotion, the intense juxtapositions of colour and rough, simple textures that he developed from his study of primitive art: these created equivalents to, rather than stylistic pastiches of, the primitive experiences: and in paintings like *The Last Supper*, 1909, *Pentecost*, 1910, or *The Life of Christ* polyptych, 1911–12 (all in the collection of the Nolde Foundation, Seebüll) we find works of a remarkable, almost sacramental quality, seemingly charged with the same spirit as the actual events themselves. Grotesquely simple and harshly painted, they leave us not questioning for one moment Nolde's assertion that, after starting to work on them in despair and doubt, he found his faith in the very act of painting.

Many other Expressionist artists of Nolde's generation produced notable religious work, in particular Schmidt-Rottluff and Kokoschka. However, it is not really until after the First World War that we find another artist, Max Beckmann, creating religiously-inspired work at this same pitch of intensity. His late-developing art was crucially affected by the First World War, the horrors of which he endured first-hand in the Medical Corps. Like Gauguin – and more relevantly, perhaps, like

Nolde – Beckmann found in the forms and the spirit of the Medieval much of relevance to his own purposes. Indeed, in many of his religious works, such as *Christ and the Woman taken in Adultery*, 1917 (The Saint Louis Art Museum), the stiff, angular shapes of the bodies and clothing, and the tall, vertical compositions reveal a medieval influence clearly, creating in turn a feeling of claustrophobia and anxiety. At this point, his art was mostly directed at themes of savage social criticism: but later, in the 1930s, Beckmann was to merge more personal, philosophical and spiritual themes in a series of gigantic triptychs. In these, for example in *Temptation*, 1937 (National Gallery of Art, Munich), the format was again designed to draw attention to the particular spiritual values that Beckmann wished to communicate, and they contain a highly personal symbolism that it is often difficult to interpret in specific terms. They might also seem irrelevant to twentieth century biblical art were it not for deliberate biblical references. Thus, in the papers beside the central chained figure in the central panel of the *Temptation* triptych can be found written the opening words of St. John's Gospel: "In the beginning was the word."

In France, the influence of post-Impressionist and Symbolist ideas in the 1880s and 1890s resulted, in the early years of the twentieth century, in the Fauvist movement, in which emphasis was firmly placed on form. Subject matter tended towards the traditional, neutral themes of landscape, still-life or figures, and these acted simply as unemotional vehicles for exploring the expressive effects of colour and pattern. There was not much interest in or need for religious subject matter in this art. The exception, of course, was Georges Rouault, very much the odd-man-out in the art of his time; for though he acquired a feeling for rich colour and bold design from his contact with the Fauvists, he equally had no interest whatsoever in their more purely aesthetic decorative concerns.

As a deeply committed Catholic and a close friend of the polemical Catholic writer Leon Bloy, Rouault had by 1904, like him, become appalled by the gross disparity in modern society between faith and works. Rouault's art became in effect the pictorial equivalent of Bloy's desire "at the dreadful close of this century where everything seems lost, to thrust at God the insistent cry of dereliction and anxiety for the orphaned multitude which the Father in his celestial height seems to be abandoning and which no longer has the strength to die bravely." For Rouault, this meant, to begin with, the depiction of the outcasts of a hypocritical society — the prostitutes, clowns, drunkards and desperately poor – and he painted them with a savage brush that showed them to be the ugliness of a sick society. Soon, with the appearance of specifically religious symbols (heads of Christ that became almost interchangeable with the heads of his clowns and poor men) it becomes clear that Rouault intended to create an image of Christ that could be closely identified with the sufferings of contemporary humanity.

Rouault's work is a curious combination of Post-Impressionism, Symbolism and German Expressionist *angst*. Indeed, the only other artist in Paris who could match and perhaps even surpass him in the strength of his depictions of biblical stories was the Russian-born Jewish artist, Marc Chagall. Chagall's art is a marvellous mixture of the naive Russian folk tradition and the most sophisticated and radical Parisian artistic ideas, and it provides a common meeting ground for Jewish and Christian religious traditions. Brought up as an orthodox Jew, he nevertheless seems to have had no problems putting to one side the traditional prohibition on making images. Indeed, he shows himself from the first to have had an intuitive, unorthodox approach to religious matters, enabling him to draw at will on both Jewish and Christian imagery. The result is an art which appeals to Jew and non-Jew alike: colourful and kaleidoscopic, as it is, full of Jewish earthiness and a love of story-telling, but tempered by a keen understanding of the need for strong design learnt from his close contact with the Cubists in Paris. His illustrations to *The Bible* (1931) show a cheerful, optimistic approach; though from time to time, as in *The White Crucifixion*, 1938 (Art Institute of Chicago) or *Exodus*, 1952–66 (Private collection), he presents images of flight and suffering of a tremendously moving and powerfully prophetic type.

Chagall's intuitive religious instincts are, on reflection, not all that far removed in spirit from those of Britain's greatest painter of biblical imagery in the twentieth century, Stanley Spencer. Just as Chagall had been brought up in a devoutly religious Jewish family background and was deeply intoned with a knowledge of Jewish religious literature, so Stanley Spencer owed much to the strong Christian family atmosphere of his Cookham childhood. Constant reading and learning by heart of passages from the Bible were a significant part of his early years; and like Chagall with his life-long remembrance of Vitebsk, the home of his youth, Bible stories became for Spencer irrevocably bound up with his feelings about Cookham. This sense of a particular place and its spirit is, of course, very much part of a wider English Romantic tradition that stretches back to Blake and Palmer. Spencer, too, received a sound technical training at the Slade, and had from the first developed a deep understanding and love for the simplicity of early Renaissance masters, such as Fra Angelico and Piero della Francesca. The outcome is again an unconventional mixture of the naive and the sophisticated. It is one, too, infused with that same sense of real struggle with traditional religious attitudes that has affected so many of the Bible's greatest twentieth century interpreters. As Spencer once wrote: "If one is sincerely trying to be a Christian, his work will be alright: but if he is like me, he will know difficulties, real difficulties". Yet; "Somehow religion was to do with me and I was to do with religion. It came quite naturally into my vision, like the sky and the rain." Looking at a work like *The Last Supper* (set in a Cookham barn), 1920 (Stanley Spencer Gallery, Cookham) or *The Visitation* (taking place in the Cookham meadows), 1912–13 (Private collection), this is not hard to believe.

One complex area still remains, and makes perhaps a fitting note on which to draw this Introduction to a close – that of abstract art as a means of biblical expression.

Geometry has always possessed an air of purity that has something of the divine about it: and in the same way, pure colour has always carried with it a rich and varying range of symbolic and spiritual connotations. The linking of the two to create abstracts of a religious or biblical kind has been a

significant thread in twentieth century art: and in this respect, Paul Nash's highly original illustrations for *Genesis* (1931) are among the first directly to portray a biblical theme in an abstract way. The extraordinary black square, melting slightly at the edges and depicting the *First Day*, is a bold attempt at using abstract art to illustrate the otherwise almost unillustratable moment of the first chaos. This is, it has to be said, an isolated effort in his art which was never again so abstract nor so specifically religious in character, and it remained until the post-war period of American art for a painter to attempt such associations on a more deliberate and consistent basis.

Perhaps not unsurprisingly in view of the large Jewish contribution to twentieth century biblical art, it was a Jewish artist, Barnett Newman, who used the idea of a 'zip' line to separate one pure field of colour from another, a pictorial equivalent to the act of creation itself. The title *Onement*, 1948 (Private collection) itself relates to a passage in the *Zohar* (a mystical Jewish work of commentary on parts of the Old Testament). This passage describes the moment of creation of life – a passage that Newman, of course, would have known well. Many of his paintings from this point on have biblical titles, at first drawn only from the Old Testament; but later works, notably the fourteen works from *The Stations of The Cross*, 1958–66 (Private collection), also have New Testament themes. *The Stations of The Cross* were created largely out of the bleak despair he had felt at the lack of understanding for his work, a despair in which he identified himself closely with Christ.

On the pages that follow are presented many quite startling and many exquisitely beautiful works, all on religious themes and all by artists of this century. Each is accompanied by biblical text corresponding to the story depicted; while on the final pages, you will find background commentary on each of the forty artists whose works are shown, as contributed by Paul Holberton. The diversity of imagery featured will, we hope, provide much fascination, showing most conclusively that biblical themes are still very much alive in art today.

NICHOLAS USHERWOOD

THE PLATES

	Page
Genesis PAUL NASH	10
Be 1 BARNETT NEWMAN	13
Adam and Eve (Temptation) MARC CHAGALL	15
Cain GEORG GROSZ	17
The Tower of Babel JOSEF SZUBERT	19
The Sacrifice of Isaac JACK LEVINE	21
Jacob Wrestling with the Angel ODILON REDON	23
The Finding of Moses JAMES ENSOR	25
Third Allegory BEN SHAHN	27
Late for Shabbat RICKY ROMAIN	29
The Dance Around the Golden Calf EMIL NOLDE	31
The Day of Atonement JACOB KRAMER	33
Levites Playing Music in The Holy Temple SHALOM of SAFED	35
The Capture of Samson LOVIS CORINTH	37
Psalm 69 ERNST FUCHS	39
Vision of Ezekiel DAVID BOMBERG	41
Judith II GUSTAV KLIMT	43
The Annunciation RENÉ MAGRITTE	45
The Nativity BERNARD BUFFET	47
The Flight into Egypt OSKAR KOKOSCHKA	49
The Baptism of Christ HENRI-GEORGES ROUAULT	51
The Expulsion of the Money-Changers EDWARD BURRA	53
Suffer the Little Children to come unto me MAURICE DENIS	55
The Good Samaritan PAULA MODERSOHN-BECKER	57
Christ and the Woman taken in Adultery MAX BECKMANN	59
The Pharisees KARL SCHMIDT-ROTTLUFF	61
The Prodigal Son GIORGIO DE CHIRICO	63
The Resurrection of Lazarus PIETRO ANNIGONI	65
The Sacrament of the Last Supper SALVADOR DALI	67
The Kiss of Judas JAKOB SMITS	69
The Mocking of Christ PETER KOENIG	71
"Ecco Homo" CHRISTIAN ROHLFS	73
Christ DAVID SIQUEIROS	75
Fragment of a Crucifixion FRANCIS BACON	77
Crucifixion II CAREL WEIGHT	79
Crucifixion PABLO PICASSO	81
The Deposition of Christ GRAHAM SUTHERLAND	83
Figure in Glory ALBERT GLEIZES	85
The Resurrection: The Hill of Zion STANLEY SPENCER	87
Apocalypse IVAN VEĆNAJ	89

In the beginning . . .

GENESIS 1,1

PAUL NASH *Genesis* 1924
Wood engravings, each 11.5 × 9 cm
except for The Void (9.5 × 8.25 cm)
Nonesuch Press/Victoria and Albert Museum, London

The Void

The Face of the Waters

The Division of the Light from the Darkness

Creation of the Firmament

The Dry Land appearing

Vegetation

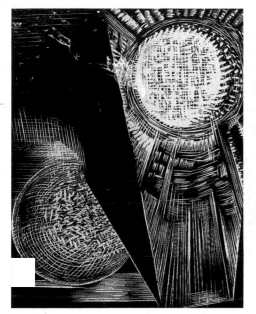

Sun and Moon

The Stars also

The Fish and the Fowl

Cattle and Creeping Thing

Man and Woman

Contemplation

Then God commanded, "Let there be light"—and light appeared. God was pleased with what he saw. Then he separated the light from the darkness, and he named the light "Day" and the darkness "Night". Evening passed and morning came—that was the first day.

Then God commanded, "Let there be a dome to divide the water and to keep it in two separate places"—and it was done. So God made a dome, and it separated the water under it from the water above it. He named the dome "Sky." Evening passed and morning came—that was the second day.

Then God commanded, "Let the water below the sky come together in one place, so that the land will appear"—and it was done. He named the land "Earth," and the water which had come together he named "Sea." And God was pleased with what he saw.

Genisis 1, 3–10

BARNETT NEWMAN *Be I (Second Version)* 1970
Acrylic on canvas, 284 × 214 cm
The Detroit Institute of Arts

Now the snake was the most cunning animal that the Lord God had made. The snake asked the woman, "Did God really tell you not to eat fruit from any tree in the garden?"

"We may eat the fruit of any tree in the garden," the woman answered, "except the tree in the middle of it. God told us not to eat the fruit of that tree or even touch it; if we do, we will die."

The snake replied, "That's not true; you will not die. God said that, because he knows that when you eat it you will be like God and know what is good and what is bad."

The woman saw how beautiful the tree was and how good the fruit would be to eat, and she thought how wonderful it would be to become wise. So she took some of the fruit and ate it. Then she gave some to her husband, and he also ate it. As soon as they had eaten it, they were given understanding and realized that they were naked; so they sewed fig leaves together and covered themselves.

That evening they heard the Lord God walking in the garden, and they hid from him among the trees. But the Lord God called out to the man, "Where are you?"

He answered, "I heard you in the garden; I was afraid and hid from you, because I was naked."

"Who told you that you were naked?" God asked. "Did you eat the fruit that I told you not to eat?"

The man answered, "The woman you put here with me gave me the fruit, and I ate it."

The Lord God asked the woman, "Why did you do this?"

She replied, "The snake tricked me into eating it."

GENESIS 3, 1–13

14

MARC CHAGALL *Adam and Eve (Temptation)* 1912
Oil on canvas, 160.5 × 114 cm
The Saint Louis Art Museum

Then the Lord said, "Why have you done this terrible thing? Your brother's blood is crying out to me from the ground, like a voice calling for revenge. You are placed under a curse and can no longer farm the soil. It has soaked up your brother's blood as if it had opened its mouth to receive it when you killed him. If you try to grow crops, the soil will not produce anything; you will be a homeless wanderer on the earth."

And Cain said to the Lord, "This punishment is too hard for me to bear. You are driving me off the land and away from your presence. I will be a homeless wanderer on the earth, and anyone who finds me will kill me."

But the Lord answered, "No. If anyone kills you, seven lives will be taken in revenge." So the Lord put a mark on Cain to warn anyone who met him not to kill him. And Cain went away from the Lord's presence and lived in a land called "Wandering," which is east of Eden.

GENESIS 4, 10–16

GEORG GROSZ *Cain* 1944
Oil on canvas, 100 × 125 cm
Georg Grosz Estate, USA

At first, the people of the whole world had only one language and used the same words. As they wandered about in the East, they came to a plain in Babylonia and settled there. They said to one another, "Come on! Let's make bricks and bake them hard." So they had bricks to build with and tar to hold them together. They said, "Now let's build a city with a tower that reaches the sky, so that we can make a name for ourselves and not be scattered all over the earth."

Then the Lord came down to see the city and the tower which those men had built, and he said, "Now then, these are all one people and they speak one language; this is just the beginning of what they are going to do. Soon they will be able to do anything they want! Let us go down and mix up their language so that they will not understand one another." So the Lord scattered them all over the earth, and they stopped building the city. The city was called Babylon, because there the Lord mixed up the language of all the people, and from there he scattered them all over the earth.

GENESIS 11, 1–9

JOSEF SZUBERT *The Tower of Babel* 1976
Oil on board, 45 × 54 cm
Zimmerer Collection, Warsaw

18

Some time later God tested Abraham; he called to him, "Abraham!" And Abraham answered, "Yes, here I am!"

"Take your son," God said, "your only son, Isaac, whom you love so much, and go to the land of Moriah. There on a mountain that I will show you, offer him as a sacrifice to me."

Early next morning Abraham cut some wood for the sacrifice, loaded his donkey, and took Isaac and two servants with him. They started out for the place that God had told him about. On the third day Abraham saw the place in the distance. Then he said to the servants, "Stay here with the donkey. The boy and I will go over there and worship, and then we will come back to you."

Abraham made Isaac carry the wood for the sacrifice, and he himself carried a knife and live coals for starting the fire. As they walked along together, Isaac said, "Father!"

He answered, "Yes, my son?"

Isaac asked, "I see that you have the coals and the wood, but where is the lamb for the sacrifice?"

Abraham answered, "God himself will provide one." And the two of them walked on together.

When they came to the place which God had told him about, Abraham built an altar and arranged the wood on it. He tied up his son and placed him on the altar, on top of the wood. Then he picked up the knife to kill him. But the angel of the Lord called to him from heaven, "Abraham, Abraham!"

He answered, "Yes, here I am."

"Don't hurt the boy or do anything to him," he said. "Now I know that you honour and obey God, because you have not kept back your only son from me."

Abraham looked round and saw a ram caught in a bush by its horns. He went and got it and offered it as a burnt-offering instead of his son. Abraham named that place "The Lord Provides." And even today people say, "On the Lord's mountain he provides."

Genesis 22, 1–14

20

JACK LEVINE *The Sacrifice of Isaac* 1974
Oil on canvas, 102 × 89 cm
Kennedy Galleries, New York

That same night Jacob got up, took his two wives, his two concubines, and his eleven children, and crossed the River Jabbok. After he had sent them across, he also sent across all that he owned, but he stayed behind, alone.

Then a man came and wrestled with him until just before daybreak. When the man saw that he was not winning the struggle, he struck Jacob on the hip, and it was thrown out of joint. The man said, "Let me go; daylight is coming."

"I won't, unless you bless me," Jacob answered.

"What is your name?" the man asked.

"Jacob," he answered.

The man said, "Your name will no longer be Jacob. You have struggled with God and with men, and you have won; so your name will be Israel."

Jacob said, "Now tell me your name."

But he answered, "Why do you want to know my name?" Then he blessed Jacob.

Jacob said, "I have seen God face to face, and I am still alive"; so he named the place Peniel. The sun rose as Jacob was leaving Peniel, and he was limping because of his hip. Even today the descendants of Israel do not eat the muscle which is on the hip-joint, because it was on this muscle that Jacob was struck.

GENESIS 32, 22–32

ODILON REDON *Jacob Wrestling with the Angel* Pre-1909
Oils, 143.5 × 62 cm
Brooklyn Museum, New York

During this time a man from the tribe of Levi married a woman of his own tribe, and she bore him a son. When she saw what a fine baby he was, she hid him for three months. But when she could not hide him any longer, she took a basket made of reeds and covered it with tar to make it watertight. She put the baby in it and then placed it in the tall grass at the edge of the river. The baby's sister stood some distance away to see what would happen to him.

The king's daughter came down to the river to bathe, while her servants walked along the bank. Suddenly she noticed the basket in the tall grass and sent a slavegirl to get it. The princess opened it and saw a baby boy. He was crying, and she felt sorry for him. "This is one of the Hebrew babies," she said.

Then his sister asked her, "Shall I go and call a Hebrew woman to act as a wet-nurse?"

"Please do," she answered. So the girl went and brought the baby's own mother. The princess told the woman, "Take this baby and nurse him for me, and I will pay you." So she took the baby and nursed him. Later, when the child was old enough, she took him to the king's daughter, who adopted him as her own son. She said to herself, "I pulled him out of the water, and so I name him Moses."

Exodus 2, 1–10

JAMES ENSOR *The Finding of Moses* 1924
Oil on canvas, 119.5 × 128.5 cm
University Art Museum, University of California

God spoke, and these were his words: "I am the Lord your God who brought you out of Egypt, where you were slaves.

"Worship no god but me.

"Do not make for yourselves images of anything in heaven or on earth or in the water under the earth. Do not bow down to any idol or worship it, because I am the Lord your God and I tolerate no rivals. I bring punishment on those who hate me and on their descendants down to the third and fourth generation. But I show my love to thousands of generations of those who love me and obey my laws.

"Do not use my name for evil purposes, for I, the Lord your God, will punish anyone who misuses my name.

"Observe the Sabbath and keep it holy. You have six days in which to do your work, but the seventh day is a day of rest dedicated to me. On that day no one is to work – neither you, your children, your slaves, your animals, nor the foreigners who live in your country. In six days I, the Lord, made the earth, the sky, the sea, and everything in them, but on the seventh day I rested. That is why I, the Lord, blessed the Sabbath and made it holy.

"Respect your father and your mother, so that you may live a long time in the land that I am giving you.

"Do not commit murder.

"Do not commit adultery.

"Do not steal.

"Do not accuse anyone falsely.

"Do not desire another man's house; do not desire his wife, his slaves, his cattle, his donkeys, or anything else that he owns."

Exodus 20, 1–17

BEN SHAHN *Third Allegory* 1955
Tempera, 95 × 63 cm
The Vatican Museum of Modern Religious Art

The Lord commanded Moses to say to the people of Israel, "Keep the Sabbath, my day of rest, because it is a sign between you and me for all time to come, to show that I, the Lord, have made you my own people. You must keep the day of rest, because it is sacred. Whoever does not keep it, but works on that day, is to be put to death. You have six days in which to do your work, but the seventh day is a solemn day of rest dedicated to me. Whoever does any work on that day is to be put to death. The people of Israel are to keep this day as a sign of the covenant. It is a permanent sign between the people of Israel and me, because I, the Lord, made heaven and earth in six days, and on the seventh day I stopped working and rested."

EXODUS 31, 12–17

RICKY ROMAIN *Late for Shabbat* 1985
Oil on canvas, 143 × 122 cm
Private collection

When the people saw that Moses had not come down from the mountain but was staying there a long time, they gathered round Aaron and said to him, "We do not know what has happened to this man Moses, who led us out of Egypt; so make us a god to lead us."

Aaron said to them, "Take off the gold earrings which your wives, your sons, and your daughters are wearing, and bring them to me." So all the people took off their gold earrings and brought them to Aaron. He took the earrings, melted them, poured the gold into a mould, and made a gold bull-calf.

The people said, "Israel, this is our god, who led us out of Egypt!"

Then Aaron built an altar in front of the gold bull and announced, "Tomorrow there will be a festival to honour the Lord." Early the next morning they brought some animals to burn as sacrifices and others to eat as fellowship-offerings. The people sat down to a feast, which turned into an orgy of drinking and sex.

EXODUS 32, 1–6

EMIL NOLDE *The Dance around the Golden Calf* 1910
Oil on canvas, 88 × 106 cm
Nolde Foundation, Seebull

The tenth day of the seventh month is the day when the annual ritual is to be performed to take away the sins of the people. On that day do not eat anything at all; come together for worship, and present a food-offering to the Lord. Do no work on that day, because it is the day for performing the ritual to take away sin. Anyone who eats anything on that day will no longer be considered one of God's people. And if anyone does any work on that day, the Lord himself will put him to death. This regulation applies to all your descendants, no matter where they live. From sunset on the ninth day of the month to sunset on the tenth observe this day as a special day of rest, during which nothing may be eaten.

LEVITICUS 23, 26–32

JACOB KRAMER *The Day of Atonement* 1919
Oil on canvas, 39 × 48 cm
Leeds City Art Gallery

All the priests present, regardless of the group to which they belonged, had consecrated themselves. And all the Levite musicians – Asaph, Heman, and Jeduthun, and the members of their clans – were wearing linen clothing. The Levites stood near the east side of the altar with cymbals and harps, and with them were a hundred and twenty priests playing trumpets. The singers were accompanied in perfect harmony by trumpets, cymbals, and other instruments, as they praised the Lord, singing:

"Praise the Lord, because he is good,
And his love is eternal."

As the priests were leaving the Temple, it was suddenly filled with a cloud shining with the dazzling light of the Lord's presence, and they could not continue the service of worship.

THE SECOND BOOK OF CHRONICLES 5, 11–14

(שלום מושקוביץ הגלילי צפת)   הַלְוִיִם מנגנים בבית המקדש

SHALOM OF SAFED *Levites playing music, in the Holy Temple* 1972
Acrylic on canvas, 61 × 61 cm
The Jewish Museum, New York

After this, Samson fell in love with a woman named Delilah, who lived in the Valley of Sorek. The five Philistine kings went to her and said, "Trick Samson into telling you why he is so strong and how we can overpower him, tie him up, and make him helpless. Each one of us will give you eleven hundred pieces of silver."

So Delilah said to Samson, "Please tell me what makes you so strong. If someone wanted to tie you up and make you helpless, how could he do it?"

Samson answered, "If they tie me up with seven new bowstrings that are not dried out, I'll be as weak as anybody else."

So the Philistine kings brought Delilah seven new bowstrings that were not dried out, and she tied Samson up. She had some men waiting in another room, so she shouted, "Samson! The Philistines are coming!" But he snapped the bowstrings just as thread breaks when fire touches it. So they still did not know the secret of his strength.

Delilah said to Samson, "Look, you've been making a fool of me and not telling me the truth. Please tell me how someone could tie you up."

He answered, "If they tie me with new ropes that have never been used, I'll be as weak as anybody else."

So Delilah got some new ropes and tied him up. Then she shouted, "Samson! The Philistines are coming!" The men were waiting in another room. But he snapped the ropes off his arms like thread.

Delilah said to Samson, "You're still making a fool of me and not telling me the truth. Tell me how someone could tie you up."

He answered, "If you weave my seven locks of hair into a loom, and make it tight with a peg, I'll be as weak as anybody else."

Delilah then lulled him to sleep, took his seven locks of hair, and wove them into the loom. She made it tight with a peg and shouted, "Samson! The Philistines are coming!" But he woke up and pulled his hair loose from the loom.

So she said to him, "How can you say you love me, when you don't mean it? You've made a fool of me three times, and you still haven't told me what makes you so strong." She kept on asking him, day after day. He got so sick and tired of her nagging him about it that he finally told her the truth. "My hair has never been cut," he said. "I have been dedicated to God as a Nazirite from the time I was born. If my hair were cut, I would lose my strength and be as weak as anybody else."

When Delilah realized that he had told her the truth, she sent a message to the Philistine kings and said, "Come back just once more. He has told me the truth." Then they came and brought the money with them. Delilah lulled Samson to sleep in her lap and then called a man who cut off Samson's seven locks of hair. Then she began to torment him, for he had lost his strength. Then she shouted "Samson! The Philistines are coming!" He woke up and thought, "I'll get loose and go free, as always." He did not know that the Lord had left him. The Philistines captured him and put his eyes out. They took him to Gaza, chained him with bronze chains, and put him to work grinding at the mill in the prison. But his hair started growing again.

JUDGES 16, 4–22

LOVIS CORINTH *The Capture of Samson* 1907
Oil on canvas, 200 × 175 cm
Mittelrheinisches Landesmuseum, Mainz

Save me, O God!
  The water is up to my neck;
I am sinking in deep mud,
  and there is no solid ground;
I am out in deep water,
  and the waves are about to drown me.
I am worn out from calling for help,
  and my throat is aching.
I have strained my eyes,
  looking for your help.

Those who hate me for no reason
  are more numerous than the hairs of
    my head.
My enemies tell lies against me;
  they are strong and want to kill me.
They made me give back things I did
  not steal.
My sins, O God, are not hidden from
  you;
  you know how foolish I have been.
Don't let me bring shame on those who
  trust in you,
    Sovereign Lord Almighty!
Don't let me bring disgrace to those
  who worship you,
    O God of Israel!
It is for your sake that I have been
  insulted
  and that I am covered with shame.
I am like a stranger to my brothers,
  like a foreigner to my family.

My devotion to your Temple burns in
  me like a fire;
  the insults which are hurled at you
    fall on me.
I humble myself by fasting,
  and people insult me;
I dress myself in clothes of mourning,
  and they laugh at me.
They talk about me in the streets,
  and drunkards make up songs about
    me.

But as for me, I will pray to you, Lord;
  answer me, God, at a time you choose.
Answer me because of your great love,
  because you keep your promise to
    save.
Save me from sinking in the mud;
  keep me safe from my enemies,
  safe from the deep water.
Don't let the flood come over me;
  don't let me drown in the depths
  or sink into the grave.

Answer me, Lord, in the goodness of
  your constant love;
  in your great compassion turn to me!
Don't hide yourself from your servant;
  I am in great trouble – answer me
    now!
Come to me and save me;
  rescue me from my enemies.

PSALM 69, 1–18

38

ERNST FUCHS *Psalm 69* 1949–60
Tempera, 75 × 50cm
Museum of Modern Art, Vienna

I felt the powerful presence of the Lord, and his spirit took me and set me down in a valley where the ground was covered with bones. He led me all round the valley, and I could see that there were very many bones and that they were very dry. He said to me, "Mortal man, can these bones come back to life?"

I replied, "Sovereign Lord, only you can answer that!"

He said, "Prophesy to the bones. Tell these dry bones to listen to the word of the Lord. Tell them that I, the Sovereign Lord, am saying to them: I am going to put breath into you and bring you back to life. I will give you sinews and muscles, and cover you with skin. I will put breath into you and bring you back to life. Then you will know that I am the Lord."

So I prophesied as I had been told. While I was speaking, I heard a rattling noise, and the bones began to join together. While I watched, the bones were covered with sinews and muscles, and then with skin. But there was no breath in the bodies.

God said to me, "Mortal man, prophesy to the wind. Tell the wind that the Sovereign Lord commands it to come from every direction, to breathe into these dead bodies, and to bring them back to life."

So I prophesied as I had been told. Breath entered the bodies, and they came to life and stood up. There were enough of them to form an army.

God said to me, "Mortal man, the people of Israel are like these bones. They say that they are dried up, without any hope and with no future. So prophesy to my people Israel and tell them that I, the Sovereign Lord, am going to open their graves. I am going to take them out and bring them back to the land of Israel. When I open the graves where my people are buried and bring them out, they will know that I am the Lord. I will put my breath in them, bring them back to life, and let them live in their own land. Then they will know that I am the Lord. I have promised that I would do this—and I will. I, the Lord, have spoken."

Ezekiel 37, 1–14

DAVID BOMBERG *Vision of Ezekiel* 1912
Oil on canvas, 115 × 138 cm
Tate Gallery, London

Finally, when it got late, the guests excused themselves and left. Bagoas then closed up the tent from the outside and prevented Holofernes' servants from going in. So they all went to bed; everyone was very tired because the banquet had lasted so long. Judith was left alone in the tent with Holofernes who was lying drunk on his bed. Judith's slave-woman was waiting outside the tent for Judith to go and pray, as she had done each night. Judith had also told Bagoas that she would be going out to pray as usual.

All the guests and servants were now gone, and Judith and Holofernes were alone in the tent. Judith stood by Holofernes' bed and prayed silently, "O Lord, God Almighty, help me with what I am about to do for the glory of Jerusalem. Now is the time to rescue your chosen people and to help me carry out my plan to destroy the enemies who are threatening us." Judith went to the bedpost by Holofernes' head and took down his sword. She came closer, seized Holofernes by the hair of his head, and said, "O Lord, God of Israel, give me strength now." Then Judith raised the sword and struck him twice on the neck as hard as she could, chopping off his head. She rolled his body off the bed and took down the mosquito net from the bedposts. Then she came out and gave Holofernes' head to her slave, who put it in the food bag.

JUDITH 13, 1–10

GUSTAV KLIMT *Judith II* 1909
Oil on canvas, 178 × 46 cm
Gallery of Modern Art, Ca'Pesaro, Venice

In the sixth month of Elizabeth's pregnancy God sent the angel Gabriel to a town in Galilee named Nazareth. He had a message for a girl promised in marriage to a man named Joseph, who was a descendant of King David. The girl's name was Mary. The angel came to her and said, "Peace be with you! The Lord is with you and has greatly blessed you!"

Mary was deeply troubled by the angel's message, and she wondered what his words meant. The angel said to her, "Don't be afraid, Mary; God has been gracious to you. You will become pregnant and give birth to a son, and you will name him Jesus. He will be great and will be called the Son of the Most High God. The Lord God will make him a king, as his ancestor David was, and he will be the king of the descendants of Jacob for ever; his kingdom will never end!"

Mary said to the angel, "I am a virgin. How, then, can this be?"

The angel answered, "The Holy Spirit will come on you, and God's power will rest upon you. For this reason the holy child will be called the Son of God. Remember your relative Elizabeth. It is said that she cannot have children, but she herself is now six months pregnant, even though she is very old. For there is nothing that God cannot do."

"I am the Lord's servant," said Mary; "may it happen to me as you have said." And the angel left her.

LUKE 1, 26–38

RENÉ MAGRITTE *The Annunciation* 1929
Oil on canvas, 114 × 146 cm
Tate Gallery, London

There were some shepherds in that part of the country who were spending the night in the fields, taking care of their flocks. An angel of the Lord appeared to them, and the glory of the Lord shone over them. They were terribly afraid, but the angel said to them, "Don't be afraid! I am here with good news for you, which will bring great joy to all the people. This very day in David's town your Saviour was born – Christ the Lord! And this is what will prove it to you: you will find a baby wrapped in strips of cloth and lying in a manger."

Suddenly a great army of heaven's angels appeared with the angel, singing praises to God:
"Glory to God in the highest heaven, and peace on earth to those with whom he is pleased!"

When the angels went away from them back into heaven, the shepherds said to one another, "Let's go to Bethlehem and see this thing that has happend, which the Lord has told us."

So they hurried off and found Mary and Joseph and saw the baby lying in the manger. When the shepherds saw him, they told them what the angel had said about the child. All who heard it were amazed at what the shepherds said. Mary remembered all these things and thought deeply about them. The shepherds went back, singing praises to God for all they had heard and seen; it had been just as the angel had told them.

LUKE 2, 8–20

BERNARD BUFFET *The Nativity* 1961
Oil on canvas, 200 × 600 cm
The Vatican Museum of Modern Religious Art

After they had left, an angel of the Lord appeared in a dream to Joseph and said, "Herod will be looking for the child in order to kill him. So get up, take the child and his mother and escape to Egypt, and stay there until I tell you to leave."

Joseph got up, took the child and his mother, and left during the night for Egypt, where he stayed until Herod died. This was done to make what the Lord had said through the prophet come true, "I called my Son out of Egypt."

MATTHEW 2, 13–15

OSKAR KOKOSCHKA *The Flight into Egypt* 1911
Oil on canvas, 55 × 68 cm
Private collection

At that time Jesus arrived from Galilee and came to John at the Jordan to be baptized by him. But John tried to make him change his mind. "I ought to be baptized by you," John said, "and yet you have come to me!"

But Jesus answered him, "Let it be so for now. For in this way we shall do all that God requires." So John agreed.

As soon as Jesus was baptized, he came up out of the water. Then heaven was opened to him, and he saw the Spirit of God coming down like a dove and alighting on him. Then a voice said from heaven, "This is my own dear Son, with whom I am pleased."

MATTHEW 3, 13–17

HENRI-GEORGES ROUAULT *The Baptism of Christ* 1911
Watercolour and pastel, 63 × 58 cm
Museum of Modern Art, Paris

It was almost time for the Passover Festival, so Jesus went to Jerusalem. There in the Temple he found men selling cattle, sheep, and pigeons, and also the money-changers sitting at their tables. So he made a whip from cords and drove all the animals out of the Temple, both the sheep and the cattle; he overturned the tables of the money-changers and scattered their coins; and he ordered the men who sold the pigeons, "Take them out of here! Stop making my Father's house a market-place!" His disciples remembered that the scripture says, "My devotion to your house, O God, burns in me like a fire."

The Jewish authorities replied with a question, "What miracle can you perform to show us that you have the right to do this?"

Jesus answered, "Tear down this Temple, and in three days I will build it again."

"Are you going to build it again in three days?" they asked him. "It has taken forty-six years to build this Temple!"

But the temple Jesus was speaking about was his body. So when he was raised from death, his disciples remembered that he had said this, and they believed the scripture and what Jesus had said.

John 2, 13–21

EDWARD BURRA *The Expulsion of the Money-Changers* 1950–52
Watercolour and body colour, 204 × 133 cm
Private collection

S ome people brought children to Jesus for him to place his hands on them, but the disciples scolded the people. When Jesus noticed this, he was angry and said to his disciples, "Let the children come to me, and do not stop them, because the Kingdom of God belongs to such as these. I assure you that whoever does not receive the Kingdom of God like a child will never enter it." Then he took the children in his arms, placed his hands on each of them, and blessed them.

MARK 10, 13–16

MAURICE DENIS *Suffer the Little Children to come unto me* 1900
Oil on canvas, 185 × 189 cm
Clemens Sels Museum, Neuss

A teacher of the Law came up and tried to trap Jesus. "Teacher," he asked, "what must I do to receive eternal life?"

Jesus answered him, "What do the Scriptures say? How do you interpret them?"

The man answered, "'Love the Lord your God with all your heart, with all your soul, with all your strength, and with all your mind'; and 'Love your neighbour as you love yourself.'"

"You are right," Jesus replied; "do this and you will live."

But the teacher of the Law wanted to justify himself, so he asked Jesus, "Who is my neighbour?"

Jesus answered, "There was once a man who was going down from Jerusalem to Jericho when robbers attacked him, stripped him, and beat him up, leaving him half dead. It so happened that a priest was going down that road; but when he saw the man, he walked on by, on the other side. In the same way a Levite also came along, went over and looked at the man, and then walked on by, on the other side. But a Samaritan who was travelling that way came upon the man, and when he saw him, his heart was filled with pity. He went over to him, poured oil and wine on his wounds and bandaged them; then he put the man on his own animal and took him to an inn, where he took care of him. The next day he took out two silver coins and gave them to the innkeeper. 'Take care of him,' he told the innkeeper, 'and when I come back this way, I will pay you whatever else you spend on him.'"

And Jesus concluded, "In your opinion, which one of these three acted like a neighbour towards the man attacked by robbers?"

The teacher of the Law answered, "The one who was kind to him."

Jesus replied, "You go, then, and do the same."

Luke 10, 25–37

PAULA MODERSOHN-BECKER *The Good Samaritan* 1906
Oil on paper, 31 × 37 cm
Formerly in the Ludwig-Roselius Collection, Bremen

Then everyone went home, but Jesus went to the Mount of Olives. Early the next morning he went back to the Temple. All the people gathered round him, and he sat down and began to teach them. The teachers of the Law and the Pharisees brought in a woman who had been caught committing adultery, and they made her stand before them all. "Teacher," they said to Jesus, "this woman was caught in the very act of committing adultery. In our Law Moses commanded that such a woman must be stoned to death. Now, what do you say?" They said this to trap Jesus, so that they could accuse him. But he bent over and wrote on the ground with his finger.

As they stood there asking him questions, he straightened himself up and said to them, "Whichever one of you has committed no sin may throw the first stone at her." Then he bent over again and wrote on the ground. When they heard this, they all left, one by one, the older ones first. Jesus was left alone with the woman still standing there. He straightened himself up and said to her, "Where are they? Is there no one left to condemn you?"

"No one, sir," she answered.

"Well, then," Jesus said, "I do not condemn you either. Go, but do not sin again."

John 8, 1–11

MAX BECKMANN *Christ and the Woman taken in Adultery* 1917
Oil on canvas, 149.2 × 126.7 cm
The Saint Louis Art Museum

When Jesus finished speaking, a Pharisee invited him to eat with him; so he went in and sat down to eat. The Pharisee was surprised when he noticed that Jesus had not washed before eating. So the Lord said to him, "Now then, you Pharisees clean the outside of your cup and plate, but inside you are full of violence and evil. Fools! Did not God, who made the outside, also make the inside? But give what is in your cups and plates to the poor, and everything will be ritually clean for you.

"How terrible for you Pharisees! You give God a tenth of the seasoning herbs, such as mint and rue and all the other herbs, but you neglect justice and love for God. These you should practise, without neglecting the others.

"How terrible for you Pharisees! You love the reserved seats in the synagogues and to be greeted with respect in the market-places. How terrible for you! You are like unmarked graves which people walk on without knowing it."

LUKE 11, 37—44

KARL SCHMIDT-ROTTLUFF *The Pharisees* 1912
Oil on canvas, 75.9 × 102.9 cm
Museum of Modern Art, New York

Jesus went on to say, "There was once a man who had two sons. The younger one said to him, 'Father, give me my share of the property now.' So the man divided his property between his two sons. After a few days the younger son sold his part of the property and left home with the money. He went to a country far away, where he wasted his money in reckless living. He spent everything he had. Then a severe famine spread over that country, and he was left without a thing. So he went to work for one of the citizens of that country, who sent him out to his farm to take care of the pigs. He wished he could fill himself with the bean pods the pigs ate, but no one gave him anything to eat. At last he came to his senses and said, 'All my father's hired workers have more than they can eat, and here I am about to starve! I will get up and go to my father and say, Father, I have sinned against God and against you. I am no longer fit to be called your son; treat me as one of your hired workers.' So he got up and started back to his father.

"He was still a long way from home when his father saw him; his heart was filled with pity, and he ran, threw his arms round his son, and kissed him. 'Father,' the son said, 'I have sinned against God and against you. I am no longer fit to be called your son.' But the father called his servants. 'Hurry!' he said. 'Bring the best robe and put it on him. Put a ring on his finger and shoes on his feet. Then go and get the prize calf and kill it, and let us celebrate with a feast! For this son of mine was dead, but now he is alive; he was lost, but now he has been found.' And so the feasting began.

"In the meantime the elder son was out in the field. On his way back, when he came close to the house, he heard the music and dancing. So he called one of the servants and asked him, 'What's going on?' 'Your brother has come back home,' the servant answered, 'and your father has killed the prize calf, because he got him back safe and sound.'

"The elder brother was so angry that he would not go into the house; so his father came out and begged him to come in. But he answered his father, 'Look, all these years I have worked for you like a slave, and I have never disobeyed your orders. What have you given me? Not even a goat for me to have a feast with my friends! But this son of yours wasted all your property on prostitutes, and when he comes back home, you kill the prize calf for him!' 'My son,' the father answered, 'you are always here with me, and everything I have is yours. But we had to celebrate and be happy, because your brother was dead, but now he is alive; he was lost, but now he has been found.'"

LUKE 15, 11–32

62

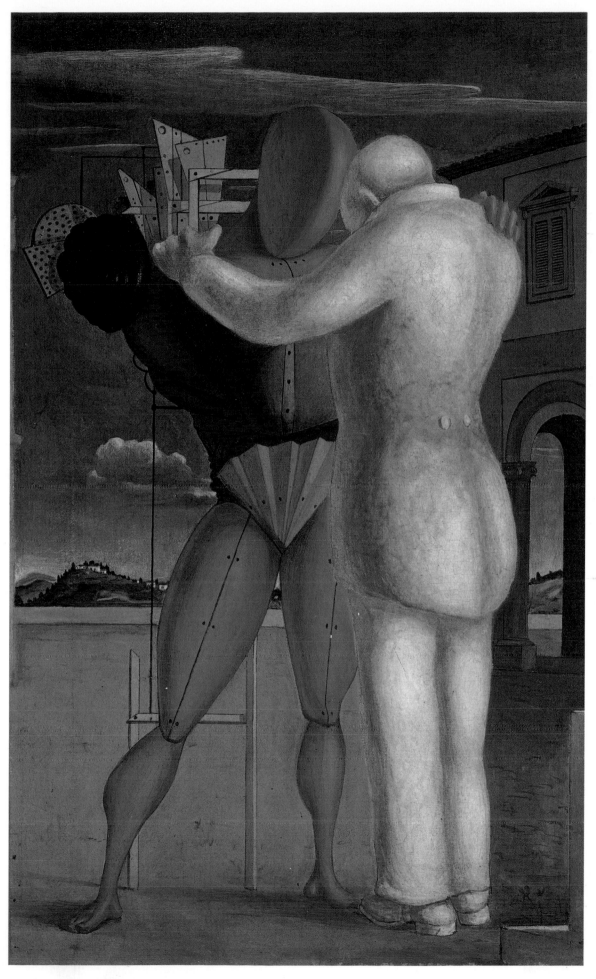

GIORGIO DE CHIRICO *The Prodigal Son* 1922 (detail)
Oil on canvas, 88.5 × 60 cm
Civic Modern Art Gallery, Milan

When Jesus arrived, he found that Lazarus had been buried four days before. Bethany was less than three kilometres from Jerusalem, and many Judaeans had come to see Martha and Mary to comfort them over their brother's death.

When Martha heard that Jesus was coming, she went out to meet him, but Mary stayed in the house. Martha said to Jesus, "If you had been here, Lord, my brother would not have died! But I know that even now God will give you whatever you ask him for."

"Your brother will rise to life," Jesus told her.

"I know," she replied, "that he will rise to life on the last day."

Jesus said to her, "I am the resurrection and the life. Whoever believes in me will live, even though he dies; and whoever lives and believes in me will never die. Do you believe this?"

"Yes, Lord!" she answered. "I do believe that you are the Messiah, the Son of God, who was to come into the world."

After Martha said this, she went back and called her sister Mary privately. "The Teacher is here," she told her, "and is asking for you." When Mary heard this, she got up and hurried out to meet him. (Jesus had not yet arrived in the village, but was still in the place where Martha had met him.) The people who were in the house with Mary, comforting her, followed her when they saw her get up and hurry out. They thought that she was going to the grave to weep there.

Mary arrived where Jesus was, and as soon as she saw him, she fell at his feet. "Lord," she said, "if you had been here, my brother would not have died!"

Jesus saw her weeping, and he saw how the people who were with her were weeping also; his heart was touched, and he was deeply moved. "Where have you buried him?" he asked them.

"Come and see, Lord," they answered.

Jesus wept. "See how much he loved him!" the people said.

But some of them said, "He gave sight to the blind man, didn't he? Could he not have kept Lazarus from dying?"

Deeply moved once more, Jesus went to the tomb, which was a cave with a stone placed at the entrance. "Take the stone away!" Jesus ordered.

Martha, the dead man's sister, answered, "There will be a bad smell, Lord. He has been buried four days!"

Jesus said to her, "Didn't I tell you that you would see God's glory if you believed?" They took the stone away. Jesus looked up and said, "I thank you, Father, that you listen to me. I know that you always listen to me, but I say this for the sake of the people here, so that they will believe that you sent me." After he had said this, he called out in a loud voice, "Lazarus, come out!" He came out, his hands and feet wrapped in grave clothes, and with a cloth round his face. "Untie him," Jesus told them, "and let him go."

JOHN 11, 17–44

PIETRO ANNIGONI *The Resurrection of Lazarus* 1946
Oil on canvas, 98 × 80 cm
The Vatican Museum of Modern Religious Art

When the hour came, Jesus took his place at the table with the apostles. He said to them, "I have wanted so much to eat this Passover meal with you before I suffer! For I tell you, I will never eat it until it is given its full meaning in the Kingdom of God."

Then Jesus took a cup, gave thanks to God, and said, "Take this and share it among yourselves. I tell you that from now on I will not drink this wine until the Kingdom of God comes."

Then he took a piece of bread, gave thanks to God, broke it, and gave it to them, saying, "This is my body, which is given for you. Do this in memory of me." In the same way, he gave them the cup after the supper, saying, "This cup is God's new covenant sealed with my blood, which is poured out for you.

"But, look! The one who betrays me is here at the table with me! The Son of Man will die as God has decided, but how terrible for that man who betrays him!"

Luke 22, 14–22

SALVADOR DALI *The Sacrament of the Last Supper* 1955
Oil on canvas, 167 × 268 cm
National Gallery of Art, Washington

J esus was still speaking when a crowd arrived, led by Judas, one of the twelve disciples. He came up to Jesus to kiss him. But Jesus said, "Judas, is it with a kiss that you betray the Son of Man?"

<small>LUKE 22, 47–48</small>

JAKOB SMITS *The Kiss of Judas* 1908
Oil on canvas, 81 × 111 cm
Antwerp Royal Museum of Fine Arts

Then Pilate's soldiers took Jesus into the governor's palace, and the whole company gathered round him. They stripped off his clothes and put a scarlet robe on him. Then they made a crown out of thorny branches and placed it on his head, and put a stick in his right hand; then they knelt before him and mocked him. "Long live the King of the Jews!" they said. They spat on him, and took the stick and hit him over the head. When they had finished mocking him, they took the robe off and put his own clothes back on him. Then they led him out to crucify him.

MATTHEW 27, 27–31

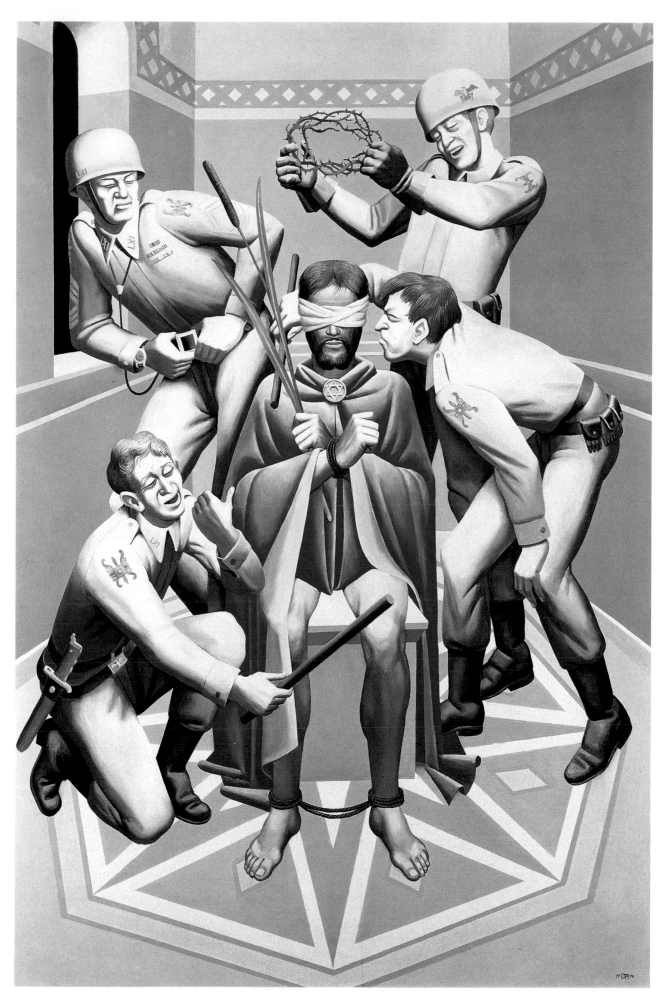

PETER KOENIG *The Mocking of Christ* 1981
Oil on canvas, 116 × 76 cm
Possession of the artist

Then Pilate took Jesus and had him whipped. The soldiers made a crown out of thorny branches and put it on his head; then they put a purple robe on him and came to him and said, "Long live the King of the Jews!" And they went up and slapped him.

Pilate went out once more and said to the crowd, "Look, I will bring him out here to you to let you see that I cannot find any reason to condemn him." So Jesus came out, wearing the crown of thorns and the purple robe. Pilate said to them, "Look! Here is the man!"

JOHN 19, 1–5

CHRISTIAN ROHLFS *"Ecce Homo"* 1922
Tempera on canvas, 101 × 80 cm
Folkwang Museum, Essen

When the chief priests and the temple guards saw him, they shouted, "Crucify him! Crucify him!"

Pilate said to them, "You take him, then, and crucify him. I find no reason to condemn him."

The crowd answered back, "We have a law that says he ought to die, because he claimed to be the Son of God."

When Pilate heard this, he was even more afraid. He went back into the palace and asked Jesus, "Where do you come from?"

But Jesus did not answer. Pilate said to him, "You will not speak to me? Remember, I have the authority to set you free and also to have you crucified."

Jesus answered, "You have authority over me only because it was given to you by God. So the man who handed me over to you is guilty of a worse sin."

JOHN 19, 6–11

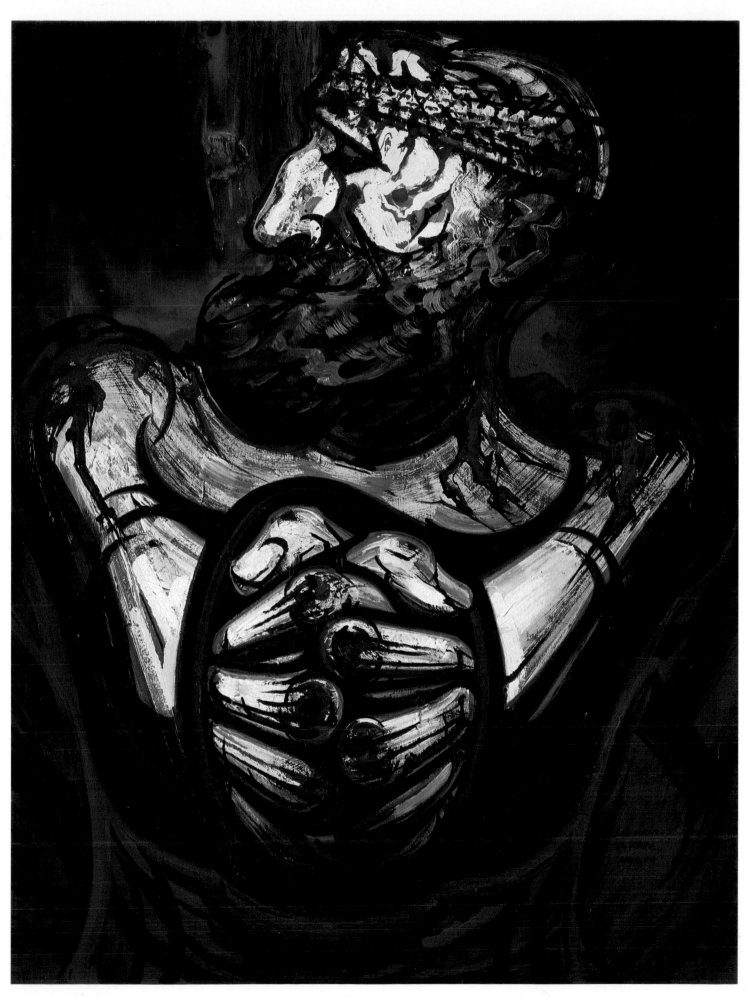

DAVID SIQUEIROS *Christ* 1970
Mixed media on wood, 182 × 145 cm
The Vatican Museum of Modern Religious Art

At noon the whole country was covered with darkness, which lasted for three hours. At about three o'clock Jesus cried out with a loud shout, "*Eli, Eli, lema sabachthani?*" which means, "My God, my God, why did you abandon me?"

Some of the people standing there heard him and said, "He is calling for Elijah!" One of them ran up at once, took a sponge, soaked it in cheap wine, put it on the end of a stick, and tried to make him drink it.

But the others said, "Wait, let us see if Elijah is coming to save him!"

Jesus again gave a loud cry and breathed his last.

MATTHEW 27, 45–50

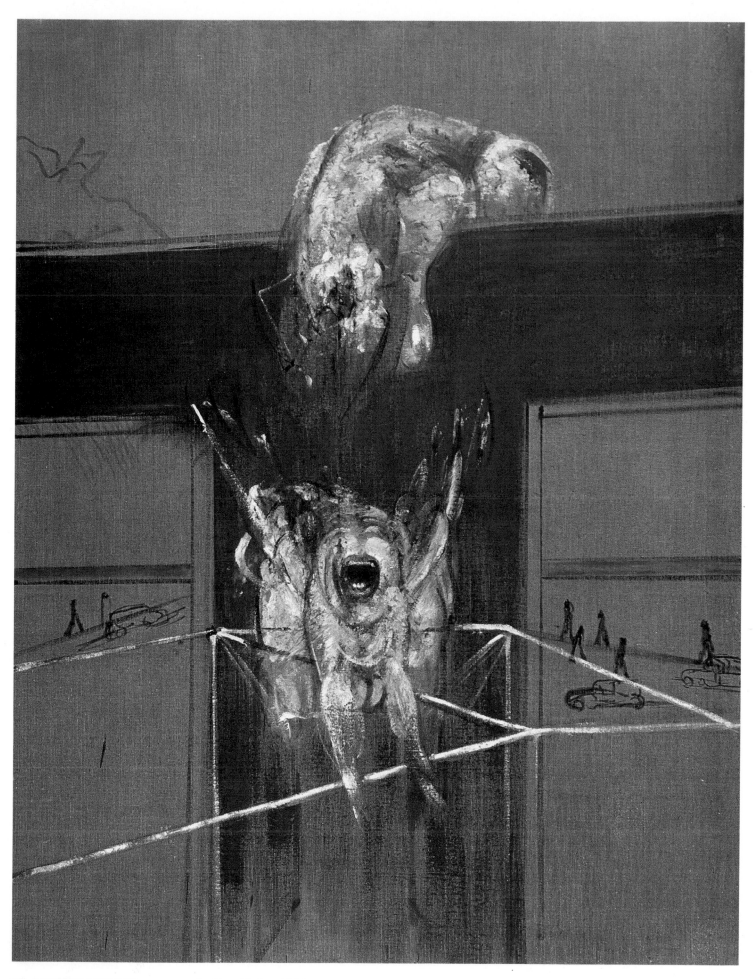

FRANCIS BACON *Fragment of a Crucifixion* 1950
Oil and cotton wool on canvas, 139 × 108 cm
Van Abbémuseum, Eindhoven

The curtain hanging in the Temple was torn in two, from top to bottom. The army officer who was standing there in front of the cross saw how Jesus had died. "This man was really the Son of God!" he said.

Some women were there, looking on from a distance. Among them were Mary Magdalene, Mary the mother of the younger James and of Joseph, and Salome. They had followed Jesus while he was in Galilee and had helped him. Many other women who had come to Jerusalem with him were there also.

MARK 15, 38–41

CAREL WEIGHT *Crucifixion II* 1981
Oil on panel, 213.5 × 111.9 cm
Duncan Campbell Fine Art

The Jewish authorities asked Pilate to allow them to break the legs of the men who had been crucified, and to take the bodies down from the crosses. They requested this because it was Friday, and they did not want the bodies to stay on the crosses on the Sabbath, since the coming Sabbath was especially holy. So the soldiers went and broke the legs of the first man and then of the other man who had been crucified with Jesus. But when they came to Jesus, they saw that he was already dead, so they did not break his legs. One of the soldiers, however, plunged his spear into Jesus' side, and at once blood and water poured out. (The one who saw this happen has spoken of it, so that you also may believe. What he said is true, and he knows that he speaks the truth.) This was done to make the scripture come true: "Not one of his bones will be broken." And there is another scripture that says, "People will look at him whom they pierced."

JOHN 19, 31–37

PABLO PICASSO *Crucifixion* 1930
Oil on wood, 50 × 65.5 cm
Picasso Museum, Paris

There was a man named Joseph from Arimathea, a town in Judaea. He was a good and honourable man, who was waiting for the coming of the Kingdom of God. Although he was a member of the Council, he had not agreed with their decision and action. He went into the presence of Pilate and asked for the body of Jesus. Then he took the body down, wrapped it in a linen sheet, and placed it in a tomb which had been dug out of solid rock and which had never been used. It was Friday, and the Sabbath was about to begin.

The women who had followed Jesus from Galilee went with Joseph and saw the tomb and how Jesus' body was placed in it. Then they went back home and prepared the spices and perfumes for the body.

On the Sabbath they rested, as the Law commanded.

Luke 23, 50–56

GRAHAM SUTHERLAND *The Deposition of Christ* 1946
Oil on millboard, 152 × 122 cm
Fitzwilliam Museum, Cambridge

After the Lord Jesus had talked with them, he was taken up to heaven and sat at the right hand of God. The disciples went and preached everywhere, and the Lord worked with them and proved that their preaching was true by the miracles that were performed.

MARK 16, 19–20

ALBERT GLEIZES *Figure in Glory* 1937
Oil on canvas, 265 × 70 cm
Musée des Beaux-Arts, Caen

Now, since our message is that Christ has been raised from death, how can some of you say that the dead will not be raised to life? If that is true, it means that Christ was not raised; and if Christ has not been raised from death, then we have nothing to preach and you have nothing to believe. More than that, we are shown to be lying about God, because we said that he raised Christ from death—but if it is true that the dead are not raised to life, then he did not raise Christ. For if the dead are not raised, neither has Christ been raised. And if Christ has not been raised, then your faith is a delusion and you are still lost in your sins. It would also mean that the believers in Christ who have died are lost. If our hope in Christ is good for this life only and no more, then we deserve more pity than anyone else in all the world.

PAUL'S LETTER TO THE CORINTHIANS 15, 12–19

STANLEY SPENCER *The Resurrection: The Hill of Zion* 1946
Oil on canvas, 94 × 190.5 cm
The Harris Museum and Art Gallery

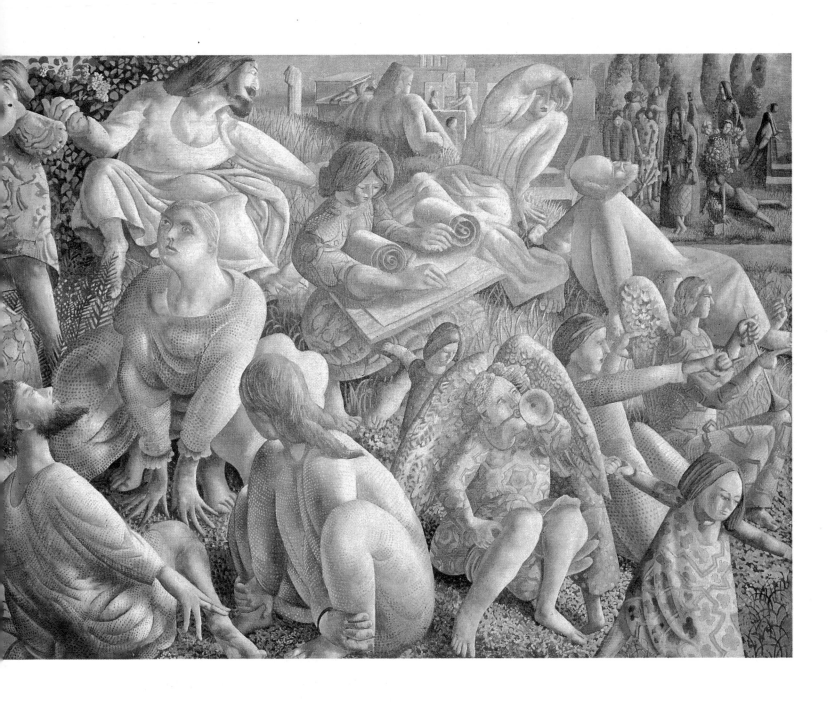

Then the sixth angel blew his trumpet. I heard a voice coming from the four corners of the gold altar standing before God. The voice said to the sixth angel, "Release the four angels who are bound at the great river Euphrates!" The four angels were released; for this very hour of this very day of this very month and year they had been kept ready to kill a third of all mankind. I was told the number of the mounted troops: it was two hundred million. And in my vision I saw the horses and their riders: they had breastplates red as fire, blue as sapphire, and yellow as sulphur. The horses' heads were like lions' heads, and from their mouths came out fire, smoke, and sulphur. A third of mankind was killed by those three plagues: the fire, the smoke, and the sulphur coming out of the horses' mouths. For the power of the horses is in their mouths and also in their tails. Their tails are like snakes with heads, and they use them to hurt people.

The rest of mankind, all those who had not been killed by these plagues, did not turn away from what they themselves had made. They did not stop worshipping demons, nor the idols of gold, silver, bronze, stone, and wood, which cannot see, hear, or walk. Nor did they repent of their murders, their magic, their sexual immorality, or their stealing.

The Revelation to John 9, 13–21

IVAN VEĆNAJ *Apocalypse* 1978
Oil on glass, 120 × 100 cm
Possession of the artist

Publishers' Note
It may be of interest that *The Capture of Samson* by Lovis Corinth,
reproduced on page 37, is signed in mirror-writing.

THE ARTISTS

Commentary by Paul Holberton

PIETRO ANNIGONI

1910–

When Pietro Annigoni held his first one-man show in Florence in 1932, he was already set on an old-fashioned, old-master kind of painting, continuing the nineteenth century norms of naturalism without even a hint of Impressionism. Though the critics complained that he was wasting his talents, his pictures did sell: and in particular Annigoni proved himself superbly adept at creating portraits of modern persons that looked as if they could appropriately be hung beside old master portraits of distinguished ancestors or predecessors.

Although he was an Italian and, despite his American mother, possessed almost no English, he was shrewdly advised that this kind of art would do especially well in England. So, in 1949, he paid his first visit to Britain in order to submit three pictures to the Royal Academy Summer Exhibition. At that time, the President of the Royal Academy was the intensely conservative Sir Alfred Munnings, who not only approved of Annigoni's pictures but praised them to the skies; and his *Self-portrait*, 1946 (Private collection), proved an enormous hit with the public, too. Indeed, Annigoni received numerous portrait commissions, and at the initiative of the City Company of Fishmongers was commissioned in 1954 to paint the portrait of the newly crowned Queen Elizabeth II. (Annigoni makes some play in his autobiography of 1977 of his perplexity that fishmongers should be involved in this royal matter.) The heavily romanticised image of the young Queen that he produced, subtly hinting at both heritage and destiny, was an unqualified success with the British population at large.

Annigoni went on to paint portraits of other heads of state, of society people, and of film stars. His output also includes landscapes and Symbolist compositions, but these have attracted much less attention. His own most serious interest has been to continue the great fresco tradition of the Italian masters; and in 1937 he was given a commission to paint a chapel in the Dominican Convent of San Marco in Florence, already famed for frescoes by the fifteenth-century artist, Fra Angelico. Since 1967, he has also been engaged intermittently in producing a series of frescoes for the church of Santa Maria di Consiglio in Ponte Buggianese, Tuscany.

Annigoni's attitude towards these various religious commissions very much corresponds to his attitude towards art. Though he does not himself believe, he feels a sense of nostalgia for religion and needs to know, as he says, that "in churches there are men who pray".

FRANCIS BACON

1909–

Francis Bacon first took up painting seriously during the Second World War, when his asthma debarred him from military service. He then emerged very suddenly into the limelight with an exhibition of 1944, in which his triptych, *Three Studies for Figures at the Base of a Crucifixion*, 1944 (Tate Gallery, London), first of all created a sensation for the violence of its imagery. Then, with the revelation of the horrors of Dachau and Belsen and other concentration camps, it was felt to be a timely expression of the darker side of human nature. But Bacon's reputation as a prophet of Nazi cruelty is not the whole story of his art; for his artistic importance consists not in *what* he paints, but *how*.

The measure of Bacon's achievement is that he should have caused so much shock despite painting in a non-naturalistic manner. Many people have even found his art deeply offensive. An immediate precedent was the Surrealist work of Paul Nash, in which objects and space are firmly organized: but Bacon uses one central element only which he frames or boxes, almost trapping it.

The dense, seemingly vicious smear of paint in the centre of Bacon's pictures is charged with life, feeling, energy, suffering, disgust, love and death – the essential aim being to create immediate impact. As he has put it: "There is an area of the nervous system to which the texture of paint communicates more violently than anything else".

With this aim in view, Bacon has often sought out newspaper photographs, action stills, medical text-books, death masks and whatever aids him in his search for what grips or compels. He discovered early on that raw meat or wounds had particular power, and also opted for the Crucifixion as an appropriate subject for impactful pictures. He painted several Crucifixions as early as 1933, and another in 1935 which he destroyed, even though it had "a very beautiful wound". After his *Three Studies* of 1944, he has on various occasions returned at intervals to the Crucifixion as a theme.

MAX BECKMANN

1904–1950

Max Beckmann was born in Leipzig, the son of a flour merchant. He studied art at the Weimar Academy, and travelled to Paris in 1904, but was soon back in Germany, where he exhibited successfully in 1906, the year in which he married. He became a member of the Berlin *Sezession*, the leading art institution, and his career continued to prosper.

World War I changed things permanently for the rising artist and his family, however. Beckmann served in the medical corps from 1914; but what was initially an exhilarating experience turned rapidly into disillusionment and horror, and to a nervous breakdown in 1915. Invalided out, the artist went to live alone, apart from his family, in Frankfurt, and began the slow process of readjustment and recovery (if there ever was a full recovery). In this process, art undoubtedly served Beckmann as a kind of therapy, but it also enabled him to express a national and European ill perhaps more profoundly than any contemporary.

Beckmann had been influenced since adolescence by the writings of Friedrich Nietzsche, receiving from them the promise of a new life, full of passion and struggle. Undoubtedly, he had seen himself as one of those who would overcome by struggle: a "superman", as Nietzsche had expressed it. But war taught him futility and defeat: and his personal nightmare, though it had a universal relevance, was expressed particularly in a painting of 1919, *Night* (Kunstsammlung Nordrhein Westfalen, Düsseldorf), probably his most famous work. It depicts a man being strangled, his wife being raped and his child being kidnapped by intruders, and is representative of the various political factions in a Germany not only war-torn but also civil war-torn. It is both a personal allegory (the strangled man is a covert self-portrait) and a searing statement of the destruction of hope.

Beckmann continued to paint such allegories, often in the form of a triptych, throughout his career, incorporating a rich variety of references – biblical, mythological and mystical. They tended to replace the religious subjects he had painted before and during the War, though these did not cease entirely. Before the War, he had even painted a Resurrection, taking place in a drawing room. He then tried to paint the same subject again, taking place in the trenches, but failed to complete it.

Beckmann painted self-portaits throughout his career, and he would be a great painter for these alone. Already in the years before the War, he had identified himself with Christ, like Dürer before him: and this identification served for him as a metaphor of the Nietzschean struggle, which he had always recognized to be full of pain but eventually triumphant. Christ's Resurrection did not mean literally salvation from death for him, but it did symbolize the breakthrough into a richer and true life.

With the coming to power of the Nazis in Germany in 1933, Beckmann was dismissed from his teaching post at Frankfurt and moved to Berlin, finally leaving Germany for Amsterdam the morning after the opening of the 'Degenerate Art' show organized by the Nazis in 1937, in which his work was prominent. Remaining in Amsterdam throughout World War II, often in adverse conditions, he moved to St Louis, Missouri, in 1947, and died in New York in 1950.

Principal religious works include *Self-portrait (as Christ)*, 1908 (Private collection), *Deposition from the Cross*, 1917 (Museum of Modern Art, New York) and *The Prodigal Son*, 1949 (Stadtische Galerie, Hanover).

DAVID BOMBERG
1890–1957

Born in Birmingham, in 1890, the son of an immigrant Jewish leather craftsman from Poland, David Bomberg was at first apprenticed to a lithographer. But after early friendships with the sculptor Ossip Zadkine and the painter John Singer Sargent, and also some lessons from Walter Sickert, he enrolled in 1911 at the Slade School of Art, London, in a celebrated class that also included Spencer.

Having demonstrated an early talent, Bomberg was, significantly, approached by an associate of the Dutch group *De Stijl*, but decided not to join this purist abstract group of which the leader, Piet Mondrian, later achieved world renown. He also refused to join the Vorticists, led by Wyndham Lewis, whose strenuous publicity stole some of Bomberg's thunder. He was, however, perhaps the most talented and interesting artist to emerge in Britain in the years immediately before the First World War, and perhaps, too, the most tragic. During the years 1912–14, in just a very small number of works – *The Mud Bath, Vision of Ezekiel*, and *In the Hold* (Tate Gallery London) among them – Bomberg developed the boldest and most accomplished response to Cubism and the abstract movements of Europe that appeared in Britain. But by standing so resolutely alone, he failed to capitalize on the early critical interest taken in his work, and after the war he suffered undeserved neglect.

Between World Wars I and II, this idealistic and committed artist was forced to attempt compromise, without real success, and even to give up painting for periods in order to teach. In 1918 he received an important commission for a Canadian War Memorial which bore, however, the proviso that his picture should not be Cubist. This attitude – constant and unshifting throughout certain sources of patronage at the time – forced him to find a new style, and this he developed in a magnificent series of landscapes painted in Palestine in the years following 1923, particularly in Petra (now in Jordan). But these works, though received well enough critically, did not sell. He was not unknown, but neither was he recognized. Bomberg himself commented: "I approach drawing only for structure; I am perhaps the most unpopular artist in England".

After the Second World War, Bomberg achieved a measure of success at the centre of two groups formed round him by his students: the Borough Group (1948–50) and the Borough Bottega (1953–55). This, however, was not sustained, and Bomberg's last years were embittered as he was largely written out of the history of the British avant-garde. Recognition of his role, of his individuality and his talent seemed on the horizon, however, when a retrospective was planned by an official body, the Arts Council, but this did not take place until 1958, the year following his death. Though he never returned to biblical subjects, Bomberg's *Vision of Ezekiel* of 1913 was reportedly one of a series of Old Testament paintings, now believed to be lost. Given the outstanding quality and power of this one remaining work, the loss to twentieth century religious art would seem to be considerable.

BERNARD BUFFET

1928–

Born in 1928, in Paris, Bernard Buffet held his first one-man show when he was just nineteen and a student at the École des Beaux-Arts. His bold and distinctive pictures were spotted by prominent Parisian art critics, and he quickly became the subject of snowballing critical acclaim which was to culminate in the joint award to Buffet and to Bernard Larjou, a much more senior and distinguished painter, of the prestigious Critics' Prize of 1948.

Buffet's work is characteristically spiky and stark in style, with limited use of colour. His work includes much by way of still-life and landscapes, but his most successful pictures are often of animals, insects or human figures in pain, shown a little or a lot over life-size. The work obviously struck a chord during the late 1940s and early 1950s, standing as it did for revolt against the establishment and for a mood of victimization or alienation among individual members of society. In a sense, he had caught the spirit of the age: and adulatory critics saw Buffet as "the passage from before to after the War". But modernist art was to progress in other directions: so that, with the new pre-eminence of New York over Paris and the establishment in the mid-50s of the avant-garde orthodoxy that good painting must be abstract, Buffet's status soon diminished somewhat.

At their best, Buffet's angular, slender figures achieve a considerable presence, as for instance in his representations of the Passion of Christ, in which they stand isolated against an empty landscape or stage, and wherein they communicate a powerful despair. There is no motion in this world without flora or fauna: only Christ's wounds and the mourners' grief.

Buffet has continued to exhibit regularly, and has shown in most European countries as well as the United States and Japan, usually choosing a theme or subject matter for each show. These themes have varied widely, and range from religious subjects to the French Revolution; and most recently, automobiles.

EDWARD BURRA

1905–1976

Although he lived to be seventy-one, Edward Burra was almost permanently afflicted by ill-health. However, in spite of this ever-present shadow physically, Burra commanded a robust and implacable spirit, defying the frailty of his body with a rare and passionate love of adventure, as can be seen in both his lifestyle and his art.

Having completed art school at the age of twenty in 1925, Burra left England, but on his return from the European mainland, where he had spent much time in France, he settled once again on Britain's south coast. He belonged to no particular school, forming a distinctive style very early: and this outlived his forays into the topical modes of his youth, such as Cubism and Surrealism. But his greatest affinity was certainly to the German movement of emphatic but unconventional Realism, dubbed *Neue Sachlichkeit* (New Concreteness), and he was influenced particularly by one of its leading proponents, Georg Grosz.

Typical of Burra are his chatty, busy crowd scenes, full of performing characters, sometimes a little larger than life, sometimes caricatured. For though Burra was seldom satirical with moral or critical intent (unlike many painters of the *Neue Sachlichkeit*), he had a keen eye for the anecdotal and for grotesque detail. However, the influence of Surrealism was to deepen his range, giving wider scope to an always active imagination: so that paintings of the later 1930s and 1940s often have a Baroque character, full of striking attitudes, great bursting clouds of colour, and grimacing figures. Thus, his *Agony in the Garden* 1938–39 (Private collection) shows Christ in his vigil of doubt and fear, rather as if he were King Lear: and his *Mexican Church* of 1938 (Tate Gallery, London) combines a fascination with the exuberant ornament of the church furnishings with a gloomy portrayal of the prominent crucifix and the black-clad widows praying before it.

In his later career, Burra returned to his favourite street and bar scenes but also ventured into landscape and still-life, in which he made a significant and timely contribution to the English tradition. In many respects, his art deserves to be compared with the novels of Evelyn Waugh, in which once again the mundane so easily becomes exotic and the comic, serious. Burra himself admired the novels of Ronald Furbank, and for him, as for Furbank, high church or Anglo-Catholic religion had a particular attraction.

In 1952, Burra exhibited a series of religious paintings in which this style was continued and developed. Paintings such as his *Expulsion of the Money-changers from the Temple*, 1950–52 (Private collection) and *The Coronation of the Virgin*, 1950–52 (Church of St. Bartholomew, Benthall) exploit the dramatic devices of Italian Renaissance and Baroque painting. (*The Expulsion from the Temple* was based, according to Burra himself, on El Greco's picture of the same subject in the National Gallery, London, and the *Coronation* borrows from Raphael).

MARC CHAGALL

1887–1985

One of the most remarkable aspects of Marc Chagall's religious work is the way in which he succeeds in filling biblical stories with a sense of fresh, sharply-observed contemporary life, a natural legacy of his Jewish upbringing with its sense of continuity. At the same time, equally important are the highly unconventional and instinctive attitudes he displays in his approach to formal dogma – the key, perhaps to the attraction of his art to Jew and non-Jew alike. This can be seen in many of his works, and markedly in *The White Crucifixion*, 1938 (Art Institute of Chicago), in which Christian and Hebrew symbols (like the crucifix itself and the seven-branched candlestick) come together in a highly moving image.

Born into a Chassidic Jewish family in 1887 in Vitebsk,

a provincial capital in Western Russia, Chagall grew up in an intensely religious background that undoubtedly had a profound impact on the subjects he chose to paint and the spirit in which he was to paint them. Thus, in earlier works (that is, those produced prior to 1914), the belief stressed by Chassidic Jews – that God is present in every manifestation of life – gives a marked religious intensity to the rabbis, wandering musicians, peasants and other characters he depicts.

Chagall's works, with their almost kaleidoscopic colours, communicate a vivid poetic quality with extraordinary immediacy: and it was this very quality which was to find its most prolific expression when he settled in Paris in 1923 after a brief and unhappy return to war-time and revolutionary Russia. Now he started on a number of superbly illustrated books for the dealer Vollard, among the most celebrated of which were the many water-colour studies and etchings for a special edition of *The Bible*. Not finally published until 1957, the sixty-six he had produced before war intervened in 1939, covering both Old and New Testament subjects, mark the beginning of a greatly increased interest in the religious and biblical subject matter that featured generally in his art throughout the 1930s.

After the war and completion of *The Bible*, with 105 illustrations in all, Chagall went on to undertake a further series, entitled *Designs for the Bible*, in which he treated subjects not included in the original edition. The coloured lithographs he produced for this are – like his paintings at this time – lighter and more optimistic than previous works which, in their grave and quiet intensity, had been characteristic of a sombre and troubled era.

The greatest and most original of his post-war religious work has, however, in the eyes of many critics, been reserved for large-scale mural and stained glass designs, the most celebrated of which are the twelve windows in the Hadassah Hospital synagogue in Jerusalem. In depicting the twelve tribes of Israel, Chagall has overcome the traditional Hebrew laws forbidding portrayal of the human figure by employing appropriate symbols. The effect is almost medieval in its rich, intense colouring, while the religious expression actually goes far beyond a purely Jewish quality, and is universal in appeal.

GIORGIO de CHIRICO
1888–1978

Having first trained as an engineer, the Italian painter Giorgio de Chirico studied art in Munich from 1906 to 1908 where he imbibed the vital influence of Arnold Böcklin, whose Symbolist work – featuring, for example, cloaked figures on journeys towards haunted places – anticipated de Chirico's own Metaphysical painting.

De Chirico's philosophy is neatly summed up in a *Self-portrait* of 1908 (Private collection), inscribed, in Latin: "And what shall I love beside the enigmatic?". Shortly after a first visit to Paris in 1911, he began producing the familiar time-stopped, expectant, almost empty streets and squares with titles such as *The Enigma of the Hour*, 1912 (Private

collection), or *Nostalgia of the Infinite* 1913–14 (Museum of Modern Art, New York), for which he was later to become so famous. Though their mood recalls both the siesta period of Italian small towns and the Symbolist painters' questions about the meaning of existence, their immediate inspiration appears to have been the projects and clutter of an architectural office: and the flags at the top of the tower dominating *Nostalgia of the Infinite*, streaming out so eerily on a windless day, are a convention of architects' drawings going back at least to Palladio.

Returning to Italy in 1915, de Chirico associated with the Italian Futurist painter, Carlo Carrà, and others, to create the Metaphysical school. They painted still-lifes (much as the Cubists were doing at the same time) in combinations and arrangements verging on the weird, in order to express the mystery inherent even in the most ordinary things (unlike the Cubists, whose concern with arrangements was strictly formal). De Chirico, however, from as early as 1919, returned to traditional subjects, such as *Hector and Andromache*, 1917 (Private collection), and the *Prodigal Son*. His several depictions of this story are painted in the same mode as his Metaphysical and pre-Metaphysical work, and the two figures, one or both of them manikins assembled from various studio objects, are always set in one of his typical half-ideal, half-deserted piazzas.

LOVIS CORINTH
1858–1925

Lovis Corinth was not religious, but some of his most effective paintings are undoubtedly the biblical compositions. He painted biblical subjects throughout his career, usually choosing scenes of violence, such as Christ's Passion and the story of Samson, in which he could display his talent for dramatic presentation, rich characterization, and originality of design.

The artist whom Corinth sought to emulate was Rembrandt, as can be seen, for instance, in what is virtually an autobiography of self-portraits, and also in the slaughterhouse scenes for which Rembrandt's *Flayed Ox* in the Louvre, Paris, was the precedent. The young Corinth also shared with the young Rembrandt a taste for costume pictures; and when, like the older Rembrandt, the older Corinth tended to state things more starkly and soberly, the results have an impressive concentration and depth of feeling.

Although he had studied both in Germany and France, he was at first little affected by Impressionism, practising a vigorous Naturalism owing much to the example of the French painter, Courbet.

Following a move to Berlin in 1901, his technique began to loosen, and by the end of the decade he was, together with Max Liebermann, the leading practitioner of the Impressionist style in Germany. He was also during this period in great demand as a society portraitist. Though neither an academic nor a conservative artist, having joined the Berlin *Sezession*, formed as an alternative to the official art institution in 1898, he sat on the committee which refused to exhibit the paintings of the Dresden Expressionist group *Die Brücke*, in 1910.

In 1911, the year when Corinth became President of the Berlin *Sezession*, he suffered a stroke that paralysed his left side. He nevertheless resumed painting in 1912; and in this last period, before his death in 1925, produced what is now regarded as his best work and in which his own suffering somehow shows. Corinth made no programmatic change of style or even of subject matter (indeed, he often repeated his old compositions), but now painted with both a new intensity of passion and greater freedom in brushwork. Numerous religious works include *Crucifixion*, 1897 (Evangelische Kirche, Bad Tolz), *The Red Christ*, 1922 (Bayerische Staatsgemälde-Sammlungen, Munich), and *Ecce Homo*, 1925 (Öffentliche Kunstsammlung, Basle).

SALVADOR DALI

1904–

Like Picasso, the only modern artist for whom he has consistently expressed respect, Salvador Dali was a child prodigy. He did not make his name, however, until he arrived in Paris from Spain in 1928, where the following year he was to be hailed as a leading innovator of the Surrealist movement. But Dali did not practise the automatism championed by the leader of the movement, André Breton – the creation of free form by the operation of the spirit, unrestrained by conscious or rational processes. Rather, he set about giving visible, naturalistic form to his dreams and to the drama of his unconscious or *Id*. (Like all the Surrealists, Dali swallowed Freudian theory whole).

His life-long love affair with Gala, previously the wife of the Surrealist poet Paul Eluard, also began in 1929. The year before, with Luis Bunuel, he had made the seminal Surrealist film *Un Chien Andalou*. He was also at this time developing his formidably preposterous artist's persona, as well as his critical theory (he could invent jargon with greater facility than many a psychoanalyst) and some of his principal themes. True to his devotion to Sigmund Freud – they met with mutal respect in 1939 – personal obsession has always played a large part in his work: and wooden crutches, soft watches, endless glowing deserts and, of course, sexual organs are some of the objects that recur and recur in his paintings, although he took up the endless desert as the perfect setting for dreams-made-concrete from a predecessor in Surrealism, Yves Tanguy. Despite a split from the official movement in 1940, he has remained a committed Surrealist throughout his subsequent career.

In a group of paintings dating from about 1946 to 1956, the occupying objects were religious symbols. Dali had not himself become religious: he once explained that from his atheist parents he had learnt nothing of God, but first became aware of God when he heard that Nietzsche had said that God was dead. However, he was interested in religious symbols precisely as symbols. The series begins with *The Temptation of St Anthony* of 1946 (Musées Royaux des Beaux Arts, Brussels), an obvious allegory of the visitation of the *Id*; and the *Christ of St John of the Cross*, 1951 (Museum and Gallery of Art, Glasgow) is a profound representation of a mystic's vision of being present beside Christ. It is actually based on a drawing of the crucifixion attributed to St John of the Cross, and was followed by *The Hypercubic Body* of 1954 (Museum of Modern Art, New York), which is not so much a crucifixion as an image of the weight of the crucifixion in the mind, and by *The Sacrament of the Last Supper* of 1955 (National Gallery of Art, Washington) which clearly attempts to represent a sensation of the presence of God.

Subsequently, Dali has returned to religious symbols only occasionally. His *Christ of Gala* (1978) (Center Art Gallery, Honolulu), for instance, is one of the stereoscopic paintings begun in the 1960s, in which surreal objects float before the beholder in full 3-D effect.

MAURICE DENIS

1870–1943

Born in 1870 in Granville, Normandy, Maurice Denis is remembered today probably rather more for the activity of his early twenties than for his subsequent career, though he continued painting, mostly decorating, until his death in 1943. At a precocious age of 20, in 1890, he sounded what was to become a call-note of Post-Impressionism. "It should be remembered that a painting – before being a warhorse, a nude or some other story – is in essence a flat surface covered with colours arranged in certain order." While writing the article in which this statement appeared, he was a member of the group calling themselves *Nabi* (meaning 'prophet' in Hebrew) and associating with Paul Gauguin and Odilon Redon, the two most important artists of the Symbolist movement.

Like Gauguin, Denis was entranced with the primitive, the simple, the pure and the natural, and enthused with a fervour to found ideal communities (much like Vincent van Gogh in the years immediately before 1890). He was also a convinced Catholic, writing at the same period: "I wish above all in my artistic life never to tarnish my Christian dignity". His development as a mature artist, as he himself saw it, consisted of a compromise between the personal and heartfelt and the 'art of the museums', and this led ineluctably to his becoming an official artist in a break with all that now seemed to him extremist.

The bulk of his output between the two world wars consisted of religious decoration – the furnishing of chapels and churches with biblical stories or religious symbols in paint and canvas or in stained glass. With Puvis de Chavannes, he could claim to have set the tone of French religious art in the first half of the twentieth century. He was, furthermore, an enthusiastic teacher and writer. In 1908 he helped his fellow *Nabi*, Paul Ranson, found the Académie Ranson, and in 1919 founded with Georges Desvallières the *Ateliers d'Art Sacré* (Workshops for Sacred Art). In the course of time, he became an authoritative pundit on art for the Catholic Church, and his writings on art culminated with a *History of Religious Art*, published in Paris in 1939.

After the death of his first wife, Marthe, in 1919, Denis remarried and in 1922 bought the Hospital of the Priory of St Germaine-de-Laye, built in the seventeenth century by Mme de Montespan, where he lived until the unfortunate accident in which he was run over in 1943. The chapel of the Priory of St Germaine, which he continued to decorate all his life, is the most important monument of his mature art.

JAMES ENSOR

1860–1949

The son of a British father and a Belgian mother, James Ensor was born in Ostend in 1860. Here, his parents ran a souvenir and carnival shop, selling chinoiserie and masks, precisely the kind of objects later to become fundamental to Ensor's imagery in the 1880s and 1890s. Indeed, masks often replace human beings in Ensor's paintings, which in their most extreme form represent a demonic world, a kind of cacophany of the imagination, through which the noise of outside reality can be heard only dimly, if at all.

After studying at the Brussels Academy, Ensor returned to his parents' home in Ostend, where he remained all his life, moving house only once. He exhibited in a small way at first with some success, and by 1883 had become a founder member of *Les Vingt* (The Twenty), the equivalent of the German and Austrian Sezessions of the same period, a breakaway group organizing exhibitions of their own work and of the latest modern art of other countries.

Though Ensor worked much in the Impressionist tradition at this time, using loose, evocative brushwork to depict scenes of everyday life, his interiors already had an unusual air of mystery, and impressions of light and air conveyed a faint odour of must. In 1883 he had painted *Scandalized Masks*, one odd figure in a mask visiting another odd figure in a mask (Musées Royaux, Brussels). But he continued also with his interiors and still-lifes (sometimes adding sinister elements to them later), even during the late 1880s and early 1890s when he was producing the vitriolic and even pathological paintings that opened up the new means of expression and which were to make his twentieth century reputation.

In 1884, all the paintings Ensor submitted to the Brussels Salon were rejected, and in 1886 he quarrelled with a fellow *Les Vingt* artist, whom he accused of plagiarism. In 1888, *Les Vingt* rejected a proportion of his pictures, and continued to do so for subsequent exhibitions until 1893, when the group disbanded. Ensor evidently felt persecuted. He came to identify himself with Christ, and painted a number of pictures showing Christ in Ensor's own situation – *Christ among the Critics*, 1891 (Private collection), and his most famous painting, *The Entry of Christ into Brussels*, 1888–9 (Museum of Fine Art, Antwerp). In this, the figure of Christ is overwhelmed by a horrendous series of ghastly visages resembling masks that present an unforgettable image of mockery and persecution. In other works, not only paintings but also prints, the jeering faces break up into little more than aggressive worms or blobs of paint that haunt the central figure.

Ensor was not the only artist at the time to explore the world of the imagination; it was a characteristic preoccupation of the Symbolist movement. But the bitterness and outrage of his art had little parallel, except perhaps in the tormented brushwork of Vincent van Gogh. Unlike van Gogh, however, Ensor was not driven to suicide, though his painting career was almost as short: and it was perhaps precisely because his persecution mania subsided that his inspiration fell away in the mid-1890s. After 1900 he painted very little indeed, although in 1911 he was visited by Emil Nolde, a worthy acknowledgement of his influence and importance for the newly-fledged Expressionist movement.

The Finding of Moses, which dates from 1924, is one of the rare works painted after 1900, although he lived till 1949. There is nothing sinister in it; on the contrary, it is a lyrical and brightly colourful evocation of the discovery by the young princess of the baby. It takes place in a meadow, and looks back to Ensor's Impressionist work, though with a freedom of form not permitted in the 1880s.

ERNST FUCHS

1930–

The paintings and prints of Ernst Fuchs belong fully in the Symbolist and partly also in the Surrealist tradition, being densely figurative, fantastical, visionary, and often orgiastic. Like Odilon Redon, Fuchs adapts old myths to his personal expression and meaning; and as a Surrealist, he evolves his figures out of mere blotches and shadows.

Born in Vienna in 1930 into the Jewish faith, Fuchs was baptized a Roman Catholic at the age of eleven through political necessity. He has, however, remained a believing Roman Catholic, dating the actual conviction of his Christian faith to 1956.

Fuchs was strongly drawn to nineteenth century engravings in his childhood, and in the late 1940s conscientiously studied the technique of fifteenth-century Flemish and German prints, which he has sometimes closely imitated. His *Mystery of the Holy Rose* (three altarpieces, including a *Crucifixion*, for a parish church in Vienna) was also painted in late medieval material – tempera and gold leaf. Intriguingly, his visions also frequently have double titles, such as *Daphne in mystic Eve*, an interlacement of nudes and foliage recalling late nineteenth century Art Nouveau, or *Eva Madonna*, an etching and aquatint of an angular nude in fifteenth-century style, holding a child in a Madonna pose.

Fuchs has explained at length the content of his latest work. His *Cabbalah* series of etchings (named after the mystic Jewish texts) are, for example, "devoted to Adam, as the personified history of God's work" and represent the "experience of the spirit of God". Thus these images represent the whole variety of human spiritual experience. The figure of Adam is derived from Leonardo da Vinci's *Vitruvian Man* drawing – a full frontal with outstretched hands. This figure is provided with different mantles or robes that symbolize Man's mystic journey through time.

Ernst Fuchs' art has been dubbed 'magic realism', but it would be more appropriate perhaps in many respects to call it 'religious fiction', by analogy with science fiction.

ALBERT GLEIZES
1881–1953

Albert Gleizes was an important theorist and practitioner of Cubist painting, exhibiting works with the Parisian avantgarde Cubist group *Section d'Or* (Golden Section) from 1912, and in the same year writing with Jean Metzinger the first ever book about the Cubist revolution. After World War I, he became equally concerned with the search for reality behind appearances, and worked constantly to evolve a Cubist style that could express the infinite and the absolute, or even the directly religious. In 1918 he had announced to his wife one day: "Something frightening is happening to me. I really believe that I am finding God again."

The son of an industrial draughtsman working in Paris and the nephew of a professional artist, Gleizes imbibed painting from the cradle. He was always as interested in teaching and organizing artists and discussing the purpose and nature of art as he was in actual painting, and was involved in the setting up of a colony of artists as early as 1906. His most famous experiment of this kind was his Moly Sabata community, founded in 1927. Convinced that technological progress was a false path causing humanity to lose sight of true values, he sought to create a self-sufficient society of craftsmen-farmers.

On the other hand, Glezies was also emphatically modern in all he did. Even for religious themes, he regarded an abstract, Cubist style as the only possible modern means. But he did not wish to jettison tradition: and the kind of compromise or synthesis he attempted can be seen in his large canvasses for the church of Ste Blanche at Serrières in the Ardèche, and in his *Descent from the Cross*, 1951 and the *Coronation of the Virgin*, 1951 (Museum of Modern Art, Paris), where the designs are closely based on medieval types, so that the subjects are instantly recognizable. The treatment of the figures themselves, meanwhile, is highly abstract – a design of shapes and colours only, with no modelling of the form.

In other works, Gleizes used pure geometry to create for the viewer a sensation of serenity in space and time, and so achieved an intimation of the divine. His rather complicated theorizing, meanwhile, about the 'rhythms' of a form subjected to geometrical transformations as if moving through time suggests that he would probably have greeted computer-generated graphics with all the enthusiasm with which he once greeted Cubism, had he lived to see this development.

Gleizes produced many lectures and essays which have considerable importance for the understanding of ideas current during this epoch; and a fitting conclusion of his career was the commission he received to illustrate the *Pensées* (Thoughts) of the Christian philosopher Pascal.

GEORG GROSZ
1893–1959

Georg Grosz is famous for his savage depictions of German society in the years immediately after the First World War and during the 1920s. His principal output consisted of drawings for the magazines published by Wieland Herzfeld, a committed socialist, and he created brilliantly convincing caricatures of the generals and capitalists widely held responsible for Germany's contemporary ills, juxtaposed in dramatic contrast to the poor and needy, as well as to those unfortunate soldiers who had been mutilated in war and who were now forgotten. The blind and crippled street matchseller is a recurrent image in Grosz as in the works of the painter Otto Dix, who was producing very similar satiric art at the same time.

In 1914 he had joined the German Army, but obtained honourable discharge within a year, finding war a profoundly disturbing experience. Back in his native Berlin, he was associated with the anarchic and nihilistic Dada movement, a jubilant and frantic reaction of young café society to the physical and moral upheaval of the war years. (Associates of the movement all received Dada names: Grosz was called 'Propagandada'). Called up to the army again in 1917, he was unable to cope with the horrors of the front, and was invalided out in the same year. From all this, he emerged embittered and cynical; his lifestyle grew increasingly immoral and, although he made a point of joining the Communist Party as soon as it was founded in Germany in 1918, he felt there was still little hope for the future.

The art that Grosz produced, both in Germany and also during his subsequent career in the United States, to where he emigrated in 1933, following an invitation to teach at a New York art school, the Art Students' League, has often been misunderstood. Socialist commentators have complained, for instance, that though he portrayed the generals and capitalists quite correctly, he had a rather stereotyped image of the working man. They also suspect that Grosz had a secret sympathy for the wicked capitalists, a sympathy that emerged more fully when he emigrated to the United States and which was ultimately responsible for a loss of power in his art after the 1920s. All Grosz's figures, however, are stereotypes, from matchseller to exaggerated Prussian general: and what is clear from his own testimony is that he hated and was disgusted with everybody and everything, despising the very human condition. Indeed, his companions in frivolous and hedonistic living were precisely the capitalists and exploiters he caricatured: and instead of being offended, they were amused and urged him on to even greater savagery.

Grosz, however, seems to have been charmed by America, where he lost some of this universal disgust and cynicism, no longer portraying life with the same bitterness, though he continued to produce certain caricatures, of Nazi jackbooters, for instance. His image of *Cain*, which shows the young man "who turned on his brother and killed him", is planted amid heaps of bodies. Here, the world's first murderer – transported to 1944 – is overwhelmed by the consequences of his own act.

GUSTAV KLIMT
1862–1918

Gustav Klimt was a leading figure of the Art Nouveau and Symbolist style of painting that swept Europe in the last years of the nineteenth and beginning of the twentieth century. However, it was not so much the style of his paintings as their overt sexuality that occasioned the controversy that surrounded him from 1900.

Though still incorporating naturalistic elements, predominantly faces and nude female bodies, Gustav Klimt gift-wrapped his portraits and symbolic figures with an entrancing surface of Art Nouveau decoration, which was often very flat and mosaic-like, thus creating a marked contrast to the solid flesh of the woman it surrounded. There were a number of parallels to this style being produced at the same time elsewhere in Europe, but distinctive to Klimt were the novelty of his decorative repertoire and its use to evoke a shimmering, glittering world of high society and *belle époque*.

Some of Klimt's best works in this manner are his portraits; other themes are Symbolist – for example, *Hope*, which shows, in the first version of 1903, now in the National Gallery, Ottawa, a rather innocent-looking but very pregnant girl in profile, amidst a swirl of proliferating motifs. Typically Symbolist also was his obsession with the *femme fatale*, rendered most famously in the first and the second *Judith* of 1901 and 1909 (Österreichische Galerie, Vienna and Galleria d'Arte Moderna, Ca' Pesaro, Venice respectively). Considerable clamour was raised about the eroticism that especially the first emanated. His critics were offended that Klimt had not called her Salome, but it can be seen that the virtuous heroine, appearing as a kind of *agent-provocateur* of Holofernes' lust, and therefore leading him to destruction, was just as valid a choice as the passionate Salome who (in Oscar Wilde's revived medieval version, not in the biblical one) took revenge on the Baptist whom she could not seduce. In the second version, Klimt's Judith appears to be even colder, while Holofernes' head is almost entirely lost in the sequinerie of her voluminous skirts.

It was this aspect of Klimt's art that had effect particularly on his younger Viennese contemporary, Egon Schiele, who imparted to it a febrile intensity lacking in Klimt himself. A later sally into another sexual encounter related in the Bible, *Adam and Eve*, 1917–18 (Österreichische Galerie, Vienna), remained unfinished at Klimt's death in 1918.

PETER KOENIG
1939–

In art, as in life, Peter Koenig is opposed to the putting up of barriers. In his vision, all things are "interwoven" in God's love. A very clear communicator, he believes there is not sufficient appreciation of the passion and experience in the Bible. The events recounted are not, he believes, mere stories nor mere symbols, and this is shown in the direct and lucid appeal of his art.

Koenig's Austrian parents settled in England in 1939, after his father had decided to open a branch in Britain of the family lace-making business. Peter was born three years later and baptized into the Roman Catholic faith, which he has never left. He studied art at the High Wycombe School of Art and Crafts, and then took up part-time art teaching for a living, making sure from the beginning that he left himself time to paint. Growing dissatisfied with the blandness of much current religious art, he soon undertook a further course of study at the Academy of Fine Art in Nuremburg, where he was interested particularly in fresco painting, returning to England in 1971.

Koenig's pictures are usually simple, clear and strongly patterned, and sometimes symmetrical. His style is that of an illustrator, and he often works using an airbrush, while painting in oil on canvas. His design, colours and imagery are carefully calculated to convey the emotional, symbolic and narrative message. *In The Mocking of Christ*, for instance, though the soldiers are depicted as contemporary American soldiers, Christ is shown as the Saviour, impassively strong and enthroned on a Star of David, and not as a suffering figure.

Since the early 1970s, Koenig has been working on a sequence of canvasses devoted to the Song of Songs, together with the Psalms, his favourite part of the Bible. There is no confusion in what he seeks to achieve: an irrevocable celebration of faith. Indeed, Koenig does not hesitate to voice the devotional joy upon which his art is founded. "As a baptized and communicating (Holy Communion) member of the Body of Christ – what a wonderful privilege/burden! I see my paintings as a 'living out', a 'making visible', a 'song of praise' of that experience. To love God! To gaze on His face! To touch His hand! His words are a love-song! My soul longs for Him. His love is better than life itself. The first commandment – to love Him – is an arrow of desire, the rapid slash of a sickle reaping corn. He is a garden in which there is a pool of reviving water when my spirit is low. He is my playful gazelle and I His fluttering dove-moth."

OSKAR KOKOSCHKA
1886–1980

Oskar Kokoschka was born of mixed Czech and Austrian parentage in Pochlarn, on the Danube, in 1886. He was educated and learnt to paint in Vienna, where his precocious talent attracted the attention of the architect Adolf Loos in 1908. Loos, according to Kokoschka, "guided me through the heaven and hell of human experience". Certainly he confirmed Kokoschka in his career as a painter, and particularly as a portraitist.

From Vienna, Kokoschka moved in 1909 to Berlin, where he worked for the influential avantgarde magazine *Der Sturm* (The Storm). It was the first of many moves made by this ceaselessly itinerant artist. In 1911 he moved back to Vienna, and in this period painted probably the best pictures of his career, including notably the *Tempest*, 1914 (Kunstmuseum, Basle), which shows two lovers in a storm of highly decorative, broken brushwork. Its inspiration is clearly the Art Nouveau and Symbolism of the leader of the Viennese school at the turn of the century, Gustav Klimt.

Though less well known, the series of small religious pictures he made immediately upon his return to Vienna is also interesting. They are painted in sombre colours, as it were through a glass darkly, and show rather remote, unclear figures in a dream landscape. Kokoschka had been baptized a Catholic, and as a boy he had sung in a Catholic church choir, but there is little indication of his adult faith. According to his autobiography, these religious pictures were painted for his mother, with whom he stayed on his return to Vienna, and were created in a mood of reflection.

After the First World War, Kokoschka was offered a job teaching art in Dresden, but in 1924 abandoned his post and embarked on restless travels, adding landscapes of the places he visited to his staple portraiture. By 1934, he could see that neither Germany nor Austria was suitable to return to, and he settled for four fruitful years in Prague, from which he was driven in 1938 to England.

He became a British national in 1947, and retained strong links with London even after moving in 1953 to Villeneuve on Lake Geneva. There, the artist who had been known in the early 1920s as 'mad Kokoschka', became a grand old man of the early avantgarde, continuing to paint his feverish portraits.

JACOB KRAMER
1892–1962

Jacob Kramer wrote of his "terrific struggle" to attain "the essence of spirituality" in a letter of 1918, while working on his most famous and successful work, *The Day of Atonement*, which powerfully achieves the "completeness" and "essential oneness" for which he strove. Representing men in prayer during the holiest day of the Jewish calendar, *Yom Kippur*, the work communicates their collective spiritual concentration in dramatically simple style.

Kramer was by origin a Russian Jew, born at Klintsy in the Ukraine in 1892, but his family emigrated when he was eight years old to England, where they settled in Leeds. Except for a period during which he studied at the Slade School of Art in London (1912–14), and active service during the First World War, Kramer spent all his life in Leeds; and he used to say that there were just as many people in the north of England sympathetic to art as there were in the capital.

At the Slade, Kramer was one of an exceptional generation which included, among others, David Bomberg, Kramer's early friend. He later came to know the sculptor Jacob Epstein, whose bronze bust of him made in 1920 and now in the Tate Gallery, London, was one of Epstein's most successful portraits. Epstein left a vivid description of his sitter: ". . . a model who seemed to be on fire. He was extraordinarily nervous. Energy seemed to leap into his hair as he sat".

Kramer was affected only to a certain extent by the modern movements of his day. However, the quest for sincerity and authenticity behind Post-Impressionism in France and Expressionism in Germany also motivated artists in Kramer's circle at the Slade, and his early work is certainly strongly primitive and simple. In works made in the years immediately after the First World War, including the *Day of Atonement*, there is also an influence from Cubism, which shows in this picture in the insistent pattern made by the row of men in their white ritual robes.

In adult life, Kramer was not an orthodox Jew, though his mother had been. His sister reported that he would "sit in empty churches and synagogues, contemplating" rather than attend the services themselves. His Jewish identity is clear, however, in such works as *Hear Our Voice, O Lord Our God*, painted in 1919 (Leeds City Art Gallery), which shows his widowed mother in anguished meditation at the news of the pogroms then being made against the Jews in Poland. During the 1920s, he painted chiefly portraits in order to make a living, but also worked on an important picture of the suffering of Christ, though he was dissatisfied with the way it turned out and subsequently had it destroyed. Kramer's output decreased over the years, but he did continue to teach and was consistently a brilliant interpreter of art.

JACK LEVINE
1915–

Jack Levine was born in Boston in 1915, of poor Jewish parents. However, thanks to several individuals who saw his talent, he was able to study art at Harvard University from 1929–1932, under Denman Waldo Ross, whose views on colour and on the history of art were to be highly influential on the young man.

Levine held his first one-man show in New York in 1939, after intermittent employment in the Federal Art Project, set up in the Depression years. In 1942, while serving as a private in the US army, he won a prize for his painting of 1937, *String Quartet* (showing just that), which was later bought by the Museum of Modern Art, New York. As the artist relates it, he was then promoted to camouflage; but more lastingly, the prize determined his subsequent career. He next received acclaim for his *Welcome Home* (Brooklyn Museum, New York), depicting a banquet in honour of America's troops returning from the Second World War. One critic called it "as subtle as it is obvious, as decorative as it is brutal". It is in fact typical of Levine's work: painted in pretty but disjointed brushwork, the figures resemble papiermaché models but they are not really caricatures. Levine merely holds up for examination, without making any comment, American bourgeois institutions, such as funerals, fashion shows and sunbathing.

Since 1945, Levine has lived in New York, though he has also taught at different establishments, mostly on the East Coast. Movements such as Abstract Expressionism and other trends of modern art have passed him by. His art belongs in the category of social criticism, though it also includes social compassion. In the later 1950s, however, he widened his range of reference to the international stage.

His *1932* (Private collection), for instance, shows Hindenburg handing over power to Hitler. The picture is also subtitled 'In Memory of Georg Grosz', whose depictions of the ruling classes in Germany after World War I are obviously an important precedent for Levine. So also is the brushwork of the Austrian artist, Kokoschka, and the Russian-born Parisian, Soutine.

As early as 1941, Levine had painted, in rather different vein, a *King David*, now in a private collection. Other Old Testament kings followed and constitute a series. Originally, Levine had in mind a memorial to his father, and the series also reflects the artist's sense of being heir to a tradition. These rather jolly but also somewhat melancholic figures represent some of Levine's best work. Further biblical scenes were painted in just the same style as the bourgeois genre scenes, and give off the same air of actors in a comedy who do not quite understand the lines. The Abraham of Levine's late *Sacrifice of Isaac* is just such a figure, too.

RENÉ MAGRITTE

1898–1967

A Surrealist painter of the inexplicable, extraordinary and mysterious, René Magritte studied painting at the Académie des Beaux-Arts in Brussels, and lived in Belgium all his life, with the exception only of the years 1927–30, which he spent in Paris. There, he established himself as a leading artist in the circle of the Surrealist spokesman, André Breton.

His career actually began, however, with his discovery in 1922 of a painting by de Chirico entitled *Song of Love*, 1914 (Private collection). It showed a bust, a rubber glove and a few other entirely disparate objects in a stage-like landscape. All Magritte's subsequent paintings were also of this kind, still-lifes exploring what he called "a secret affinity between certain images". In a later phase, he also produced baffling juxtapositions not only of several things, but of the same thing as an object, as a word and as an image. This phase apparently began about 1928–29, with his famous *The Air and the Song* (Private collection), a picture of a pipe with the words beneath, 'This is not a pipe'. Another example is *The Human Condition 1*, 1933 (Private collection), in which an easel with a painting of a landscape is at the same time a window through which the landscape (a 'real' landscape?) is seen.

Magritte saw and stated very clearly that his pictures were not 'art'. According to his own account, de Chirico's picture enabled him to see that painting could be poetic, not a matter of style. For Magritte, the image had a value exactly equivalent to a word: it designated. Just as a poet uses words to express something in a poem, so Magritte used images to make something visible in his pictures. The beauty, for him, lay in the meaning, not in the way a word is pronounced nor in the way an image is painted. Magritte always painted in a naturalistic, almost photographic style; so that, for example, the *image* 'train' would mean 'train' just as clearly as the *word* 'train' means 'train'.

Magritte was interested only in unknowable mysteries, and departed from the known, as he said himself, in order to advance towards the unknown. At the same time, his intriguing titles are not designed to aid the baffled viewer: on the contrary, they are intended to prevent the viewer from getting used to the pictures, and essentially raise questions. Thus, his *Annunication* is also designed to raise a question as to what is being announced – be it a 'secret affinity' between the assembled objects, or an incarnation.

In 1930, the year after the painting had been completed, Magritte quarrelled with the aggressively atheist Breton over an offensive remark made by Breton to Magritte's wife because she was wearing a crucifix. This was the reason why Magritte left Paris. Quite possibly, Magritte's interest in the unknown overlapped with religious feeling.

PAULA MODERSOHN-BECKER

1876–1907

Paula Modersohn-Becker was one of the most progressive painters in Germany of her time, though this talent was virtually unrecognized during her life, even among close acquaintances. However, with the posthumous printing of some of her letters and diary entries in 1917, she became more famous; while critical acclaim for her art (over five hundred paintings and seven hundred drawings, despite her short life) came more gradually.

Born in 1876 of a cultured and bourgeois family in Dresden, Paula Becker initially complied with parental pressure to train as a teacher but went on, despite their disapproval, to study at the Berlin School of Art for Women in 1896. From 1897, she was based near Bremen, at Worpswede, home for a flourishing community of landscape painters. Among them, she met Otto Modersohn whom, though some years her senior, she was to marry in 1901.

The Worpswede School owed much to the French painter of rural life, Jean-François Millet, and their art was at this time still largely unaffected by the impact of the Impressionists. They were less interested, however, in making a record of nature than in portraying "the biblical simplicity" of the local peasantry, as Paula Becker was to express it in her diary.

First visiting Paris in 1900, Modersohn-Becker became increasingly attracted to the city itself, finding the atmosphere at Worpswede stifling by contrast and her marriage something of a disappointment. In 1903, in the company of the German writer Rilke, she visited Rodin, who was to become one of the many French artists – among them, Cézanne – to influence her progression, during the last years of her life, towards an ultimate goal of aesthetic simplicity.

By 1906 the result was evident in a style characterized by bold, crude forms in rich and heavily laid-on colour. Her style reveals, too, a major debt to Gauguin, and constitutes a striking parallel to the *Die Brücke* Expressionists, who had formed their group in Dresden in 1905. By contrast to the *Die Brücke* style, however, Modersohn-Becker's forms were more rounded and her use of colour more lighthearted. Tragically and unexpectedly, twelve days after giving birth to her only child, in 1907, she suffered an embolism and died at the very brink of her artistic maturity.

Modersohn-Becker painted mainly still-lifes, landscapes and genre scenes, usually featuring peasant women, children or a mother and child together. She once wrote that she had seen in the aspect of a peasant woman with her young child an unknowingly "heroic" figure. It was in fact an age of searching for heroes, and Modersohn-Becker found them in that kind of solid tenderness. Her little picture of the *Good Samaritan*, though almost a unique biblical subject in her mature work, is obviously concerned with this same quality, as is her *Annunciation*, 1905 (The Vatican Museum of Modern Religious Art).

PAUL NASH

1889–1946

Paul Nash was born in 1889 of an established English family, related to the writer and water-colourist, Edward Lear. Studying in London, he was one of an exceptionally talented intake at the Slade School of Art that also included David Bomberg and Stanley Spencer. He first exhibited in 1911, but his career was to be established by sketches made while on active service in Flanders during the First World War, as a result of which he was appointed an official War Artist in 1917.

The paintings made at the end of World War I and immediately after it are an outstanding record of its ravages. In works such as *Menin Road*, 1919 (Imperial War Museum, London), for instance, Nash depicts not the human horrors of the front directly but their results, landscapes of blasted mud flats and broken stumps of trees under a baleful sky. These paintings were thus not a record of a particular time and place, but a stylized or semi-abstract summary of experience: and although they show awareness of modern movements, such as Cubism, and even though the landscapes are very obviously organized into a strict design of abutting diagonals, facets and planes, they are nevertheless still recognizably landscapes.

This semi-abstract structuring of nature remained typical of Nash throughout his career, though he constantly experimented, always seeking a breakthrough into a more daring vision. The symbolist direction of Nash's work was further influenced in the mid-1920s by de Chirico and Dali. By contrast, however, with Dali, Nash remained interested in structure; and if he set strange objects impossibly together in a landscape, crucial to it was always their abstract relationship.

In 1933, he formed a short-lived but important group, *Unit One*, with the sculptor Henry Moore and others, designed specifically to remedy the lack of structural purpose in British fine art of the time. All these aspects of Nash's work are still present in his pictures painted during the Second World War, when he was again an official war artist. The most famous of these is his *Totes Meer* (Dead Sea), 1940–41 (Tate Gallery, London), a semi-abstract landscape or vision of crashed German planes.

The wood engravings illustrating the first chapter of Genesis which the Nonesuch Press published in 1924 are also outstanding. These twelve black and white images, in patterns of varying geometric complexity, evoke a remarkable sense of movement; and though abstract, they suggest an impression of the elemental forces stirring at the dawn of time. The expressive power that Nash was able to accomplish through such relatively simple compositions is one of the more striking features of his versatile talent.

BARNETT NEWMAN

1905–1970

Barnett Newman was born in New York in 1905, of Jewish parents newly arrived in America from Poland. He came to painting gradually, and the significant role he played in the development of Abstract Expressionism, the dominant movement in painting in the 1950s, was not fully recognized until 1958, when he held his first retrospective exhibition, with a catalogue by the influential critic, Clement Greenberg.

He painted very large canvasses, consisting only of an arrangement of colours and containing within their vast surfaces either single or various patterns, but nothing that could be called a figure or a form. Like his fellow Abstract Expressionists, he sought spiritual or metaphysical self-expression through these works; but individually he concentrated on exploring the relationship between a very narrow stripe of colour (which he called his 'zip') and a much larger expanse of colour. These works are among the most exhilarating and impressive products of the New York School of Abstract Expressionism.

In common with other Abstract Expressionists, among them Jackson Pollock, Newman felt it necessary to make a new start, to paint, as he said, "as if painting were not only dead but had never existed". He also shared an interest in American Indian ritual and artefacts. These, the Abstract Expressionists found, helped them achieve a way of painting that was pure, authentic and unadulterated by civilization, and through them they could jettison those establishment or cultural values that repressed the artist's 'voice'.

The Abstract Expressionists also liked to draw a parallel between the trances of the *shaman* (medicine man) when performing magical ceremonies, and their own mental state in the creation of their canvasses – whether this was in the violent action painting of Jackson Pollock or Barnett Newman's long meditations, lasting days or even weeks, over the placement of his 'zip'.

Newman identified the spiritual dimension of his art with the sense of exhilaration he experienced when a painting came out to his satisfaction. Painting was for him the creation of a special 'place'. As he put it: "What matters to the artist is that he distinguish between a place and no place at all, and the greater the work of art, the greater will be this feeling. And this feeling is the fundamental spiritual dimension".

The very titles of his paintings often indicate this specific spiritual intention, and works of the late 1940s and early 1950s include *Adam* (Tate Gallery, London), *Abraham* (Museum of Modern Art, New York), and a number of works referring to Genesis. The high-point came with the *Stations of the Cross*, a series of fourteen canvasses, now in a private collection, which Newman began painting in 1958 and finished and exhibited for the first time in 1966. This was a mere four years before his death in 1970. Newman saw the series as a progression towards the fundamental question asked by Christ on the Cross: "My God, My God, why have You forsaken Me?", or in Newman's terms, "the question that has no answer". This series naturally invites comparison with the series of abstract canvasses which Mark Rothko, Newman's friend from 1931, painted for a chapel in Houston (1967–69). Both series were designed to entrance the viewer, to immerse him an open-ended, undefined meditation, as in a state that might essentially resemble religious experience.

EMIL NOLDE

1867–1956

Of peasant birth and largely self-taught, Emil Nolde is one of the founding figures of German modern art. His surname was originally Hansen; but he adopted a new name, taking it from the town where he was born, near the German border with Denmark. Training first as a carpenter and cabinet-maker, he painted his very first canvas in 1897, at the age of 30. Having made some money from a print of the Matterhorn mountain depicted as a bearded, smiling head, he then travelled and went to art school, emerging into prominence with a painting of *Harvest Day*, 1904 (Private collection) exhibited by the break-away *Sezession* group in Berlin. Shortly afterwards, a group of artists calling themselves *Die Brücke* ('The Bridge'), later to become famous as the founders of German Expressionism, were greatly impressed by his use of colour and invited Nolde to join them. Too solitary an individual to remain for long, he stayed with them for just a few months: an encounter as fruitful for *Die Brücke* as it was encouraging for Nolde, whose output of paintings soon markedly increased.

Nolde was now 40, and though he had only just found his artistic way himself, he became almost instantly the grand old man of the German avantgarde, enthusiastically received, too, by the even more important Expressionist group, *Die Blaue Reiter* (The 'Blue Riders'), named after one of Wassily Kandinsky's paintings. Nolde's peasant birth and lack of education undoubtedly had a special appeal for the artists of these movements, keenly interested as they were in both primitive and folk art. He represented for them the key qualities of sincerity and purity, so much so that the *Blaue Reiter* Paul Klee called him, on the occasion of a great retrospective exhibition for his sixtieth birthday in 1927, an "earth spirit".

Ensor and van Gogh were both important influences, as can be seen in the extraordinary energy Nolde's canvasses convey, though the energy is in the startling, living colour rather than in the brushwork. For Nolde, painting was all about inspiration and unconscious forces. "In art I fight for unconscious creation. Labour destroys painting". Hence, in one of his famous early works, *Wildly Dancing Children*, 1909 (Kunsthalle, Kiel), motion of colour fuses with the motion of their dance: the dance *is* their colour.

In 1909 Nolde fell seriously ill, and soon afterwards there followed an irresistible desire to represent profound spirituality, religion and tenderness, "without much intention, knowledge or deliberation", as he recalled later. He painted both Old and New Testament scenes – *The Last Supper*, 1909, *Pentecost*, 1910, *Dance round the Golden Calf*, 1910, a cycle of the *Life of Christ*, 1911–12 (all held by the Nolde Foundation, Seebull) and a marvellous triptych of the legend of *St Mary of Egypt*, 1912 (Kunsthalle, Hamburg) among them. This body of work terminated with an *Entombment* (Nolde Foundation, Seebull) in 1915, though Nolde did go on to paint the occasional religious scene afterwards. At this time, he also produced biblical etchings, and created in 1912 a haunting woodcut, *The Prophet*, which has a mountainous force recalling his early Matterhorn fantasy, but without the smile.

After travelling all over the world in the years immediately before World War I, Nolde increasingly remained at home in the wild flat country where he was born, eventually settling at Seebull, where the Nolde Foundation, set up after his death in 1956, holds an enormous collection of his work. This includes the "pictures I didn't paint", made after he had been banned from taking up a brush by the Nazis in 1941. This ban was imposed following Nolde's own persistence in seeking acceptance by the Nazi Party of Expressionist art, after it had earlier been rejected.

PABLO PICASSO

1881–1973

Long before his death in 1973, Pablo Picasso was already widely regarded as the greatest artist of the twentieth century. The perennial charm of his early Blue Period and his historic contribution to the epoch-making style of Cubism, as well as the wit and spirit of his later work, won him this commanding position, which still seems unassailable today.

Born in 1881 in Malaga, Spain, Picasso was the son of a drawing master named José Ruiz. Picasso was in fact his mother's name, adopted shortly before leaving for Paris, in 1900, where he was to remain until after the Second World War was over.

During his Blue Period which lasted from 1901 to 1904, his pictures were characteristically palish blue in colour and sentimentally blue in mood, showing lonely or single figures in timeless detachment. He then moved on to rather warmer subject matter in a Rose Period, but already in 1906 had started work on the now famous *Demoiselles d'Avignon*

(Museum of Modern Art, New York), the picture that was to set him on the path to the abstract method of painting known as *Cubism*. Intending to paint a monumental nude, similar to a kind done before by Paul Cézanne, Picasso could not resist interweaving a couple of African masks for heads, and thereby found himself challenging the whole principle of representation.

For the next few years, Picasso worked in close association with Georges Braque, from whose picture *Houses at Estaque*, 1908 (Rupf Foundation, Berne), featuring houses shown as cubes, Cubsim got its name. Both artists progressed together, painting their way towards ever greater levels of abstraction. First, in a phase which became known conventionally as *Analytical Cubism*, they took a subject, typically a still-life such as a guitar, which they fragmented into numerous views or facets, and arranged representatively on the canvas. In a subsequent phase, known as *Synthetic Cubism*, the picture itself was the subject. Here they used not only shapes and colours, but also words or letters, bits of newspaper, wallpaper and wood to make similar, still-life arrangements.

After a visit to New York in 1917 where he worked on theatre designs, Picasso widened his range, returning to figure subjects. He usually painted these in an obviously abstract, Cubist style, but also worked more naturalistically. His work was regarded favourably by the Surrealists, dominant in France during the 1920s, but Picasso never tried to paint the unconscious or the inconceivable as they did. Instead he derived his forms from direct experience. But 'direct' does not mean 'simple' or 'literal', and his work was always rich in visual puns. As Picasso himself put it: "A green parrot is a green salad but also a green parrot".

Picasso endorsed the statement of André Breton, 'spokesman' for the Surrealists, that "Beauty must be convulsive": and during summers spent in the South of France from 1925 onwards, he created increasingly violent and monstrous distortions, telling Roland Penrose (his later biographer) that he had thought of embedding razor-blades in the edges of his work *Guitar*, 1920 (Kunstmuseum, Basle), "so that whoever went to lift it would cut their hands".

Picasso's *Crucifixion* was painted in 1930, when the artist himself was depressed, between love affairs, and sought a subject in which he could convey an extreme pitch of suffering. Significantly, the sketches for the picture, dating back to 1927, began with Mary Magdalene, represented, traditionally, as a sexual figure. There is little sign of this in her final form, however, at the bottom of the ladder on the left of the picture. But the painting did not reflect a religious conversion: rather, a personal anguish.

The gaping jaw with sharp teeth situated on Christ's chest is a forerunner of similar forms to be found in *Guernica*, 1937, perhaps the most powerful picture Picasso ever painted. Here, Picasso's anguish and violence were harnessed in the condemnation of an atrocity, the murderous bombing of the town of Guernica during the Spanish Civil War. (The picture has now been moved, as Picasso stipulated that it should be when democracy came to Spain, to the Prado, Madrid).

By the time of *Guernica*, Picasso had already turned decisively to sculpture, though he did not work from a solid material but constructed, mostly from metal. After the Second World War, he moved to the South of France, and extended his activity to pottery, which to some degree he revived as an art form. Meanwhile, his painting included a notable series of reworkings of famous pictures by old masters. However, while the legend grew and grew, and his often witty production continued to delight, his capacity to surprise diminished. Even so, he retained to the end an unrivalled sureness of touch, as well as humour.

ODILON REDON
1840–1916

Though committed to art from adolescence, Odilon Redon was almost forty before he made his mark in 1879, with his first edition of etchings, entitled *Dans la Rêve* (In Dream). These and subsequent lithographs evoked compelling imaginative and even, to some, sinister and compulsive vistas. As Redon himself put it, they were wanderings "on the limits of the imperceptible, that intermediate state between animal and plant life, of flower or being, that mysterious element which is animate for a few hours of the day but only under the action of light".

Redon refused, indeed did not know how to explain what his art represented, but once remarked significantly that he hated the blank page. "I am forced to scrawl on it. . . . and this operation brings it to life. I believe that suggestive art owes much to the stimulus which the material itself exerts on the artist." What Redon himself called "suggestive" art is today dubbed "Symbolist", but Redon perhaps more than any other Symbolist anticipated later Surrealist explorations of the back mind.

It was thanks to enthusiastic reviews and a Redon cult started by the Symbolist writer Huysmans that Redon first became prominent. But while Huysmans had praised the imaginative quality and rather overstressed the sinister in Redon's art, Degas admired ". . . his black, oh his blacks. . . . impossible to pull any of equal beauty". Redon was later, at the very end of the nineteenth century and the beginning of the twentieth, also able to create comparable textures in colour, starting with brilliantly coloured, luminous, and sometimes quite otherworldly flowers, and then taking over into oils and pastels some of the motifs of his lithographs.

In 1895 Huysmans had become a Roman Catholic, and though Redon did not follow him that far, he seems to have undergone a religious crisis at about the same period. He had also, in 1889 and 1890, met and befriended the religious-minded Nabi group, among them Maurice Denis: and further religious influences were exerted on him by patrons, notably Gustave Fayet, a collector also of Paul Gauguin, who commissioned an important and typical work of his later career, the series *Night, Day* and *Silence*, for the library of the former Abbey of Fontfroide, near Narbonne. These monumental half-forms, adrift in a plasma of rich colour, almost pulsate with mystical feeling.

Most of Redon's financial and critical support during the early years of the twentieth century came from Catholic circles, and Redon was certainly regarded in his own day as a religious artist, often adding biblical references to his repertoire of mythological, botanical and apocalyptic imagery. Major religious works include *Head of Christ appearing over Sea*, pre-1905 (Wittenstein Gallery, New York) and *Flight into Egypt*, 1900 (Private collection).

Redon was a modest, amiable and unbusinesslike artist, whose achievement was only partially recognized in his lifetime. Yet the deep darks of his lithographs and the pollen-like colours of his later oils and pastels remain unsurpassed.

CHRISTIAN ROHLFS

1849–1938

Following a fall from a tree when only a very young man, Christian Rohlfs was confined to bed for two whole years, an occurrence which rapidly turned him into something of a contemplative spectator of the world. He was able to take up painting, however, training briefly in Berlin, and later in Weimar: but in 1874, as a delayed consequence of the accident, his right leg had to be amputated.

Throughout his youth, Rohlfs worked unremittingly but in considerable poverty and isolation, painting the countryside round Weimar. His handicap naturally meant that he could not easily travel, so that the first time he actually saw an Impressionist painting was in 1897, when three pictures by Monet were exhibited in Weimar. Though his own style had by coincidence been progressing in that direction already, Monet's fresh colour and direct response to his subjects were a revelation: and the middle-aged painter now began a remarkable development in which he enthusiastically absorbed the most modern trends in art: Impressionism and Neo-Impressionism, then Fauvism and Expressionism.

His fortunes also changed. From 1901, Rohlfs had the support of Karl Ernst Osthaus, a young millionaire dedicated to the diffusion of the benefits of modern art; and in the following year, he was appointed Professor of Art at the Weimar Academy, though he now made his home in Hagen, where Osthaus had founded his Folkwang (Folk Hall) for modern art.

Rohlfs' principal work, consisting of landscapes and still-lifes, dates from the later part of his career. In 1905, he became influenced by the free brushwork and colour of van Gogh, and his work grew to be still more free and colourful when in the same year he met Nolde, who was of peasant birth like himself. This influence was decisive, and Rohlfs' art now came to resemble the style of the up-and-coming Expressionists, blocking out form in great strokes and pressing it hard against the frame as if it were too big for it. However, he was always more lyrical than the *Die Brücke* Expressionists such as Schmidt-Rottluff, and his colouring and form were consistently softer in contrast and outline. During the course of this first decade, he also adopted

tempera rather than oils, achieving a greater transparency of colour.

The outbreak of the First World War was to prove traumatic for Rohlfs. At first he stopped painting altogether; but then, from 1915, turned to religious subjects, as Nolde had done before him, and as Schmidt-Rottluff was to do shortly afterwards. He was not moved by religious experience, however: rather, he felt the need to represent the crisis of his unprecedented times in terms of old values, sometimes pessimistically, as in *God marks Cain*, 1919 (Private collection).

The period after World War I was mostly a happy time for Rohlfs: and in 1919, aged 70, he married for the first time. He travelled, and spent the summers at Ascona in Italy, continuing to paint landscapes and still-lifes, and the occasional figure scene. But he lived to see his works mocked and reviled in the Nazi 'Degenerate Art' exhibition of 1937, and many of them were destroyed.

RICKY ROMAIN

1948–

Ricky Romain has emerged as an artist of strong and original vision, painting the spiritual in everyday life. He has exhibited as a Naive, partly because he is self-taught, taking up painting for the first time aged 27, in 1975, and partly because his art "speaks from the heart", but his technical accomplishment and clarity of purpose put considerable strain on this label.

Born in London in 1948, Romain was brought up as a liberal rather than a strictly orthodox Jew. He came back to his faith, however, and particularly to Chassidic Judaism, largely through meditation and through other cults that were diffused in England from the late 1960s onwards. Nevertheless he still distrusts the institutional side of religion and takes an active interest in faiths other than the one into which he was born – Buddhism, for instance. But he is now observant in his own way, and the painting *Late for Shabbat* depicts the experience of himself and his family discovering that they have got behind in their preparations for the eve of the Sabbath. The table is not yet laid, the candles are not yet lit, nor the appropriate blessings made, and the sun is already going down.

Romain first came to painting after seeing the work of the Impressionists and Post-Impressionists. Colour is the basis of his art, conveying feeling, though not explicitly symbolic. His paintings may recall Chagall, but his work, though visionary, does not involve Chagallesque distortions of anatomy and scale. His paintings show real people – himself and his family, for instance – though they portray a world not resembling reality in a narrow sense. Often, too, they communicate great joy.

An important subject for Romain soon after he started painting was the story of Jacob. This embodies for him much of what it means to be a Jew; and although he has since moved to a more direct depiction of spiritual experience, the theme of Jacob is one to which he believes he may well return.

HENRI-GEORGES ROUAULT
1871–1958

Henri-Georges Rouault was a Roman Catholic throughout his life, participating in a scheme of the convert writer J.K. Huysmans to found an artist's colony in a Benedictine monastery in Belgium in 1901, and finding direct inspiration for his art from the writing of the Catholic zealot, Leon Bloy. He was also a leading figure of the French avant-garde, emerging into prominence with the *Fauve* (or 'wild') painters in the Paris Salon d'Automne of 1905.

Born in Paris of artistic but not wealthy parents in 1871, Rouault decided to follow an apprenticeship in glass-making, with study at the École des Beaux-Arts in Paris, where he was to become the favoured pupil of Gustave Moreau. Before becoming a *Fauve* in 1905, he had won official recognition and a prize, for his *Christ among the Doctors*, 1894 (Unterlinden Museum, Colmar), which reveals the formative influence not only of Moreau but also of Rembrandt.

Rouault often chose such themes as judges and tribunals, and painted winding-down circuses and joyless prostitutes: and although they are often portrayed as monsters, there is often a palpable charm and tastefulness to be found in the glowing, ember-like colours with which these figures are painted.

A growing reputation in avant-garde circles was assured when the dealer Ambroise Vollard took him up in 1917, or even, according to some accounts, shut him up in his house for a long period of assiduous production lasting into the 1930s. Vollard at first encouraged Rouault's satiric vein with a series of etchings of Alfred Jarry's comic hero, Ubu; but the dominant project became the *Miserere*, a series of 58 aquatints, sent to the press severally between 1922 and 1927. *Miserere* (meaning 'Have pity') is taken from the refrain repeated in the Mass: *Miserere nobis Domine* (Have mercy on us, Lord). The aquatints were based on sketches made during the First World War; not, however, at the front. They reflect the spiritual rather than the physical horror of war, and were originally entitled *Miserere et Guerre* (Have pity, and war), the word 'war' being dropped at the suggestion of Rouault's close friend at this time, the religious poet, André Suarès. In these aquatints, Rouault's jeering and jeered-at characters take on a still more powerful and starkly tragic quality as they bend their bowed, jet-black outlines under the seemingly enormous pressure of enclosing space. There is no colour, and the texture is oppressive.

Perhaps the most important development in Rouault's art during the 1930s was his venture into landscapes. Many of these were biblical, either incorporating a specific biblical incident, or representing a biblical landscape of the mind, such as *Autumn, Nazareth*, 1948 (Vatican Museum of Modern Religious Art). In some, his *cloisonné* or enamel colours take on a particular freshness and even an exhilaration. In figure compositions, meanwhile, he turned increasingly to Christ himself, for whose torments his developed style of muffled agony was ideally suited: and in 1939 he issued, again for Vollard, a book of 17 etchings and 82 woodcuts representing the Passion.

SHALOM OF SAFED
1885–1980

Shalom of Safed was born Shalom Moskovitz in Galilee, Israel (then Palestine) in 1885. Until his retirement in the early 1950s, at some 70 years, Shalom had been an artisan silversmith and watchmaker who practised his craft in the little town of Safed almost all his life. He was discovered in 1953 by the Israeli painter, Yossel Bergner, who taught him to paint in acrylics: and Shalom soon began producing pictures in a characteristically flat, almost 'cut-out' style that were to be exhibited and sold in New York, Chicago, Paris, Zurich, Jerusalem, Amsterdam, Stockholm, London, Detroit, Washington, Düsseldorf, Bonn and Munich from 1961 to 1987.

A true Naive, Shalom of Safed had no training or even knowledge of art. He was also a strictly orthodox Jew; and if his work had in his own eyes contravened the law against graven images he would not have done it. Indeed, he once remarked scornfully: "I am a serious man. I don't find the subjects in my imagination. Everything I do comes from the Holy Books."

The eager market for his laboriously produced works did not alter his style of life. He continued to go to the synagogue three times every day, and to paint for the same ten hours each day that he had once worked as a watchmaker.

His work consists exclusively of illustrations of the Old Testament, and he always regarded "the picture that turns men's thoughts from God by challenging His creation" as evil. Rather, he saw himself as an instrument, no more, by which God's words could be reproduced, a philosophy which is very much in accord with the theory and tradition of Semitic sacred calligraphy.

KARL SCHMIDT-ROTTLUFF
1884–1976

Karl Schmidt-Rottluff was one of the initiators of twentieth century German Expressionism. Born Karl Schmidt in the village of Rottluff near Chemnitz (now Karl-Marx-Stadt) in Saxony in 1884, Schmidt trained not as an artist but as an architect in Dresden from 1905. In the same year he formed, with others, the artists' group called *Die Brücke* – a name taken from a reference by the philosopher and prophet Nietzsche to a bridge (Brücke) from an old, stale life towards a new and richer one. He and Kirchner were the leading members of this first manifestation of Expressionism in German art, and tension between their very different personalities was a main cause of the dissolution of the group in 1913.

It was also on Schmidt's initiative that contact was made with Emil Nolde. When he visisted Nolde in 1906, Schmidt was painting in a style closely modelled on Vincent van Gogh, as a *Self-portrait* that has remained in Nolde's collection (Nolde Foundation, Seebull) very clearly shows. It has van Gogh's heavy, rapid brushwork, laid on in a rather disorganized fashion. Under Nolde's influence and that of French *Fauvism*, Schmidt simplified his handling and struck out for very bold, very basic forms in heavily charged, violently discordant colours. Expressionistically, Schmidt sought in this way to give the form a greater force or presence in his pictures than it possessed in visible reality.

In 1911 the group moved to Berlin and established contacts all over Germany. They exhibited together for the last time in Cologne in 1912, when Schmidt showed four relief *Evangelist Heads* (Private collection) in painted brass.

In 1912 Schmidt had also painted *The Pharisees*, which perhaps more than any other picture by him shows the influence of Cubism. But though such images hint at Schmidt-Rottluff's ideal of a new society, they do not express longing for it with quite the same fervour as the series of religious woodcuts begun in 1917, as a reaction to the ordeals of the First World War. Schmidt was actually fortunate enough not to see very much active service at all: so that the woodcuts relate more to the profound disquiet that war was fostering in German society.

After 1919, when he concluded the series of woodcuts with an image of St Francis, Schmidt-Rottluff returned to landscapes, still-lifes and portraits and even to decorative art, no longer painting subjects with a 'message'. He remained in Germany despite the Nazi government, and despite the fact that twenty-five of his pictures were exhibited for mockery and revulsion in the Nazi 'Degenerate Art' show in 1937. In 1941, he was officially forbidden to teach or to paint. When bombed from his home in Berlin in the same year, he returned to the village of Rottluff, and lived in what became East Germany until his death in 1976.

BEN SHAHN

1898–1969

Throughout his life, Ben Shahn – a painter of the poor, the exploited and the victimized – was continually animated by the ethics he drew out of the Bible, particularly from Ecclesiastes, the Psalms and the Prophets. Though he was not a practising Jew, he had been brought up in an Orthodox household and the Bible was in his blood, his religious feeling and social conscience being closely interwoven.

Born of Jewish parents in 1898 in Kovno, Lithuania, and emigrating with them to New York when he was eight, Shahn had his first success with a series of twenty-three gouache paintings dating from the early 1930s. These told the story, or Passion, of the unjust conviction for murder and execution in 1927 of Nicola Sacco and Bartolomeo Vanzetti, poor immigrants like the artist himself. The style of simple but vivid, almost cartoon narrative and the obvious social conscience, rooted in the conviction of "positive values", as the artist called them, were to remain typical of Shahn throughout his career. He did not, however, take up these causes at the time, but sought to make a memorial of the victim in the aftermath of the event. In this respect, he can be seen very much as a grass-roots history painter.

The causes commemorated in this way culminate in a series of eleven paintings, dating from 1961, of the destruction of a Japanese fishing-boat, the *Lucky Dragon*, destroyed by accident in an H-bomb test in 1954. By this time, Shahn's style had developed from social realism to what he called "personal realism", amounting in effect to a kind of poetic licence in the treatment of a story. His art had also expanded in other ways. Under the Public Works of Art Project initiated by the United States Government during the Depression, he began a life-long series of murals for public buildings, working in 1933 as an assistant to the Mexican muralist, Diego Rivera. Equally significant was his production of lithographs and other prints, some of which appeared separately, some in books. Meanwhile he was also becoming a homespun spokesman for his own, for American, and for modern art in general; and his most famous journalistic essay is perhaps *The Shape of Content*, 1957.

Late in life, he turned back to the Bible (but not to an exclusively Jewish outlook – his wife reports that he was also very much moved by Roman Catholic services) and produced what at first were pure calligraphic exercises, developing the characters of the Hebrew script. He then moved to semi-symbolic and semi-narrative illustration, notably in *Ram's Horn and Menorah* (Private collection) of 1958, accompanied by the Hebrew script of Malachi 2,10: "Have we not one father? Has not one God created us?" Illustrations to Ecclesiastes appeared in a book of 1965, and his lithographs of decorative lettering celebrating Psalm 150, the *Hallelujah Suite* (published by Kennedy Graphics, New York) appeared posthumously in 1971. These last are among his finest works, and are extremely seductive examples of his masterly use of decorative colour and skilful pattern-making.

DAVID SIQUEIROS

1896–1974

David Siqueiros was born the son of a lawyer and the grandson of a soldier at Chihuahua in Mexico, in 1896. He was himself a soldier and a journalist, indeed a revolutionary, before he was an artist; and throughout his long career was alternately in and out of favour with the Mexican government, by whom he was imprisoned twice. His release from prison in 1964 was, however, succeeded by a later government-sponsored retrospective exhibition in 1975. It was, of course, far easier to honour this uncompromising and inconvenient political artist after he was dead.

After fighting on the side of the successful revolutionary government, Captain Siqueiros left for Europe in 1919, to learn painting. He absorbed some of the ferment of modern art in Paris, but was active particularly in Barcelona, where he published a manifesto on the proper (revolutionary) direction of painting.

In 1922, he returned to Mexico, and undertook his first murals, benefiting from the example and friendship of the elder Mexican Muralists, Diego Rivera and José Clemente

Orozco, though he was soon to express his disagreement with both. Between 1925 and 1930, he gave up art altogether for the sake of trade union politics, and took up painting again only when he was imprisoned in 1930. During the 1930s, he was an important presence in the United States. In Los Angeles in 1932, his murals aroused interest despite their strident politics; and in New York, in 1936, his Experimental Workshop was attended by the future Abstract Expressionist, Jackson Pollock, among others. His most productive period, nevertheless, dates from after World War II.

His style is lurid and energetic but essentially naturalistic, and conceived as a challenge to Michelangelo. (His *March of Humanity in Latin America*, to be seen in the Parque de la Lama, Mexico City, was boasted to be more than three times the length of the Sistine Chapel ceiling). There is no denying the energy, but the praise lavished on Siqueiros by the Russian film-maker Sergei Eisenstein in 1932 may now seem to be somewhat double-edged. "Siqueiros is the best proof that a really good painter has, above all, a social consciousness and an ideological conviction. . . . Siqueiros strikes a blow with his brush with the implacable certainty of a pneumatic drill."

As in the patent reference to the Crucifixion in his Plaza Art Center, Los Angeles mural of *Tropical America* (an Indian is shown on the Cross under the American eagle), Siqueiros quite frequently borrowed from biblical imagery to make his political points, and the depiction of suffering in his allegories was clearly derived from the Spanish and Latin American tradition of religious art.

JAKOB SMITS

1856–1928

Jakob Smits had a restless early career. Dissatisfied with the teaching at the Academy of Fine Art in Rotterdam, he enrolled in academies at Brussels, Munich, Vienna and Rome, but returned to Rotterdam, still dissatisfied and in need of earning his living. He became a successful interior decorator like his father, and soon made an advantageous marriage. However, by the end of the decade he had divorced and then settled across the Belgian border in the district around Antwerp, where he was to remain until his death in 1928.

On moving, he turned decisively to painting, and in art and life subsequently rooted himself with fervent devotion to the still primitive peasant life of the land. His third wife, whom he married in 1901, was herself a peasant, rather than one of the bourgeoisie.

During his early career, Smits painted landscapes and the peasantry in a realist style, much like other painters in Holland at the time, particularly those of the so-called Hague School. After 1900, however, he turned more to interiors, in which he depicted still, squat forms sitting in huddled peace, emanating an earthy intensity. The prototypes for these pictures were similar interiors by Rembrandt (mostly drawings rather than paintings), but the colours in which they were painted – most notably his use of yellow – strongly recall Vermeer. He also drew from both masters in his handling of light, for him the essence of painting. "Light is a material", he would say: and he painted these peasant scenes in the most luminous colours he knew, but always with a very dense, and very visible impasto surface, in which he said he sought to be "fresher than an old Persian carpet and harmonious in the violent and fresh tones".

A Humanist, Smits also painted a number of biblical pictures, in which his subjects were once again of peasant stock. Old-fashioned simplicity was for him sacred: but in his art, as in life as a whole, he seems to have felt grossly misunderstood, and even said, when speaking of his work *Salome*, c.1908 (Collection Hotel Charlier, Saint Josse ten Node), that it was his own head on the platter, served up as his enemies would like to see it.

STANLEY SPENCER

1891–1959

Stanley Spencer took up art not for art, but in order to express his religious or quasi-religious vision, and throughout his career showed little interest nor liking for the progressive movements in modern painting.

The basis of this vision was the representation or re-creation of a childhood eye-view of his native village. Cookham, about thirty miles from London, where he was born in 1891. Spencer was unworldly, unassuming, and clumsy in his relationships. As he put it himself: "The only really significant love affairs I have ever had have been with places, rather than with human beings".

The main body of Spencer's early work consists mostly of a series of monumental religious and non-religious paintings set in Cookham. "The instinct of Moses to cast off his shoes when he saw the burning bush was very similar to my feelings. I saw many burning bushes in Cookham." Then in 1927 he began some mural canvasses for the Sandham Memorial Chapel which also feature prominently a recurrent theme of his work, the resurrection of the dead. These decorations, running all round the chapel, reveal Spencer's remarkable ability not simply to handle crowded compositions but also to infuse them with a kind of communal spirit.

After the completion of this work in 1932, Spencer was worried that he was losing his vision and only felt again more secure with a commission from the War Office in 1940 to paint works with *Shipbuilding on the Clyde* (Imperial War Museum, London), a series in which this community spirit was again appropriately and magnificently expressed. He also continued, both before the Second World War and after, to paint religious themes, most famously in an open-ended series intended for a notional Cookham church. These express his intense faith in ordinary life, and an increasing search to portray its inherent mystery. Among them are *Christ carrying the Cross*, 1920 (Tate Gallery, London), *The Crucifixion*, 1921 (Art Gallery and Museums, Aberdeen), and *A Village in Heaven*, 1937 (City of Manchester Art Galleries).

GRAHAM SUTHERLAND
1903–1980

Having trained in art at Goldsmith's College, London, Graham Sutherland then concentrated on etching and engraving, making his name quite quickly as a print-maker, and bringing out his first etchings in 1923.

However, the Depression years rapidly removed the largely American market for prints, and Sutherland therefore took up commercial design, and also painting. In 1935, encouraged by Paul Nash, he turned decisively to landscape painting, and following a visit to Pembrokeshire in 1934 which had entranced him, he was soon to make a national and, after World War II, international reputation with his typical evocations of the countryside of Wales.

The most important model for these landscapes, he revealed, was the nineteenth century artist, Samuel Palmer. Sutherland had been "amazed at its completeness, both emotional and technical", when he saw one of Palmer's etchings for the first time. Palmer's works are certainly some of the most intense expressions of the entire English school of landscape painting, and it was very much the poetry of the countryside that Sutherland set out to capture. As he put it: "It became my habit to walk through, and soak myself in the country". He did not, however, work on the spot, preferring to make sketches and producing paintings "recollected in tranquillity", to use Wordsworth's very definition of poetry.

Sutherland had become a Roman Catholic in 1926: and in 1944, he was commissioned to paint a *Crucifixion* to be placed together with the sculptor Henry Moore's *Madonna* in St Matthew's, Northampton. Meditating on Christ's Passion, Sutherland became fascinated by the thorns of the Crown of Thorns, and this gave rise to his *Thorn* pictures, a long-running series of semi-abstract meditations on the nature of thorns. The Northampton commission led, too, to a much more important commission: in 1952, he was asked to design a colossal tapestry as the altar retable for the new Coventry Cathedral. Sutherland also became known for his portraits, beginning with one of the writer Somerset Maugham in 1949. He subsequently painted other prominent figures, including Sir Winston Churchill (1954), but Lady Churchill was to burn it in disgust.

Other religious commissions also followed. It is clear, however, that Sutherland had other concerns besides the proper and effective depiction of the narrative event in his religious paintings. He was very concerned, for instance, with balance. As he said: "I wanted the figure to be real, yet not real. I wanted it to be slightly ambiguous." It was indeed an attempt to represent a traditional image in a truly modern way.

JOSEF SZUBERT
1898–1984

In 1973, at the age of seventy-five, Josef Szubert was provided with oils, brushes and primed board and ordered to start painting. A son's faith in his father's instinctive feeling for colour and composition was rewarded by the result: a charming and individual picture of two people collecting mushrooms; and Szubert's subsequent pictures soon aroused the interest of the curator of the local museum at Torun and of many other patrons of Polish folk art.

Szubert later regretted that he had not been ordered to start painting earlier: and, encouraged by his success, found the years he spent painting the most enjoyable of his whole life, despite his age.

He had been born in the village of Wrocklawki, near Chelmno, Poland, in 1898, one of seven children of the local blacksmith, and was a life-long Roman Catholic. After World War I, he became a professional soldier in the Polish army; and his taste for art was manifested during this time in the coloured technical drawings of artillery which he made for trainees while a sergeant.

During the Second World War, Szubert joined the Resistance, was arrested and sent to a concentration camp. He survived, but the years after the War were also difficult, and he held a number of jobs including locksmith, storekeeper and nightwatchman. It was only after he retired in 1970 that he took up painting, soon turning from everyday scenes to biblical themes, finding it a way in which to give thanks for safe delivery from the concentration camp. His remarkably simple, clear and sure depictions of many Bible stories reflect a lifetime's reading and re-reading of the Bible, while their serenity reveals little of the hardship of his physical life, or even of the cramped conditions in which they were painted – a small one-bedroom flat in a tower-block in Torun.

Szubert's painting career spanned just eleven years; but though short, it represents a notable achievement, for his colourful, exuberant and exquisitely composed paintings are among the finest examples of truly Naive art to have been discovered in recent times.

IVAN VEĆENAJ
1920–

Ivan Većenaj belongs to the famous Hlebine School of Naive painters in Yugoslavia, centred round the town of that name, near to Zagreb, and famous for its depiction of peasant life.

Većenaj was encouraged and taught the rudiments of painting by the founder of the Hlebine School, Ivan Generalić: but he is untypical in his concentration on biblical subject matter, although he has also painted portraits, as well as vivid landscapes. His colours have an unusual intensity: bright colours are the rule in Naive art, but Većenaj gives them a lurid, almost hallucinatory quality. Indeed, his work is sometimes almost visionary. In a typical allegory, for example, he presents birds painted in symbolic colours instead of the tablets of the Law, each bird representing a different commandment. The rooster is thus the Tenth Commandment (Thou shalt not covet thy neighbour's wife), while the Promised Land behind stands for a better life.

Born in 1920, Većenaj received only four years schooling.

He worked first as a peasant farmer, and did not take up painting until well into his thirties, after he was married and had a family. Acutely aware of the tradition in the life of which he is part, Većenaj has produced a great many pictures in his native landscape which reflect not just what the Bible tells, but also his own deeply rooted Roman Catholic faith and that of the community. In several paintings, for example, he places Jesus in an Eastern European landscape. "I put Jesus on the cross because that is the way it is in the Bible, but I placed him in the Podravina region."

CAREL WEIGHT
1908–

"There are so many subjects in the Bible that are wonderful really but I can't say that I am a religious person, I never go to church. I suppose one is religious really because one can't evade it." These sentiments, expressed in an interview with Norman Rosenthal of the Royal Academy of Arts, London, in 1981, reveal much of the British artist Carel Weight's attitude to his own religious paintings. Religion, with its treasury of themes and images, is an important vehicle for Weight's work, but he guards against voicing any strong belief. It is the human element in such subjects that inspires him – even so, some of Weight's most notable paintings are treatments of biblical episodes.

The spiritual quality of many of his works has occasionally invited comparison with another British painter, Stanley Spencer, whose idiosyncratic and visionary world seems to have an equivalent in Weight's paintings.

But while Weight himself acknowledges a certain similarity with Spencer, it is a comparison which he rightly plays down. Weight's vision is more worldly, and more empathetic, too, with the human condition. The people in his paintings seem unwittingly to express both the tragic and the comic in life, faces and attitudes caught somewhere between the sublime and the ridiculous. Weight is not a high-brow (indeed, intellectuality in art is something he rather likes to mock); and yet, surreptitiously, his paintings achieve an unexpectedly elevating effect.

In the 1930s, Weight visited an exhibition in London of works by the Norwegian expressionist painter, Edvard Munch. Soon afterwards, he became a friend of the exiled Austrian painter, Oskar Kokoschka. Both were relatively unknown in Britain at the time, but their influence on Weight is readily apparent, particularly in the energetic freedom of brushwork and, above all, use of colours. These have become progressively more intense and expressive as Weight has matured: as he himself has said, "I always wish that there were about half-a-dozen more colours that we could use." Though Weight never ventured into abstract art, he nonetheless accomplished that very modern technique, alien to most British artists of his generation, of designing pictures in colours.

In Weight's later output, religious themes have received increasing attention; but if there is anything which has truly enjoyed a devotional status in the work of this former Professor of Painting at the Royal College of Art, London, it is painting itself. Such devotion can clearly be seen in many of his large canvasses; monumental and original works which are sure to remain – in the words of his long-time friend and fellow-painter, Ruskin Spear – "superb milestones in the history of English painting".

GLOSSARY

Compiled by Julius Nelki

Abstract Art This form of art reflects the belief – voiced first by the ancient Greeks, but particularly prevalent in the twentieth century – that arrangements of colours and forms, independent of subject, possess all the aesthetic values necessary to constitute art. Semi- and pure abstraction have figured highly in modern painting and sculpture. *See also Abstract Expressionism; Cubism; Stijl, De;* and *Vorticists.*

Abstract Expressionism This form of purely abstract or non-representational art, in which the artist seeks to unlock the creative powers of the inner or subconscious mind by arranging forms or colour without reference to any subject, has been prevalent since the end of the Second World War. Major *Abstract Expressionists* include Jackson Pollock, Mark Rothko and Barnett Newman (*see* page 101). *See also Abstract Art; Action Painting.*

Action Painting This technique involves the energetic splashing and dribbling of paint on to a surface in order to create an abstract image. It is a form of *Abstract Expressionism*, practised by such artists as Jackson Pollock. *See also Abstract Expressionism.*

Analytical Cubism This second phase of *Cubism*, lasting from approximately 1909 to 1912, involved the idea of methodically breaking down an object and spreading out its various aspects on to a canvas. It was pursued with less interest in colour than earlier *Cubism* and rather more concern for crude, unadulterated form. *See also Cubism.*

Art Nouveau Emerging originally as a decorative style of architecture and interior decoration in the 1890s, the florid and naturalistic designs of *Art Nouveau* (literally 'new art') became especially popular in Britain and Belgium, where James Ensor (*see* page 96) was associated with the growth of the movement. Its influence can also be seen in the work of Gustav Klimt (*see* page 98), as with a large number of other turn-of-the-century artists.

Baroque This was a style of heavily ornate art and architecture of the late Renaissance, prevalent from the end of the sixteenth and into the eighteenth century.

Bauhaus An innovative German school of architecture and applied arts, the *Bauhaus* was founded in 1919 by Walter Gropius.

Blaue Reiter, Der Chosen by Wassily Kandinsky and Franz Marc as the name for a loosely-formed group of *Expressionist* painters, which they founded in Munich in 1911, *Der Blaue Reiter* (literally 'The Blue Rider') included, along with *Die Brücke*, the most important exponents of modern art in Germany prior to 1914. *See also Expressionism.*

Brücke, Die This was the name (literally 'The Bridge') taken in 1905 by a pioneering group of German *Expressionist* painters, among them Ernst Kirchner and Karl Schmidt-Rottluff (*see* page 105). *See also Blaue Reiter, Der.*

Cubism This style of painting, first exhibited in Paris in 1907, was developed by Georges Braque and Pablo Picasso (*see* page 102) as both an intellectual and aesthetic solution to the problem of representing a whole object on a two-dimensional surface. By juxtaposing several different views of one object, they created an art form which considerably influenced contemporary painting and from which much of twentieth century art has evolved. *See also Analytical Cubism; Synthetic Cubism.*

Dada An immediate forerunner of *Surrealism, Dada* (the French word for 'hobby-horse') was a nihilistic response to the First World War. Anarchic, and vehemently opposed to art and reason, the Dadaists deliberately set out to shock, offend and ridicule European society and its values. *See also Surrealism.*

Expressionism In this simplified style of painting, line and colour are often distorted or exaggerated in order to express an intense emotional sensation. In modern art, the principal *Expressionists* were usually German or Nordic – Max Beckmann (*see* page 91), James Ensor (*see* page 96), Emil Nolde (*see* page 102), Oskar Kokoschka (*see* page 98) and Karl Schmidt-Rottluff (*see* page 105) among them. *See also Blaue Reiter, Der; Brücke, Die.*

Fauves, Les This was the name given to a number of French artists, among them André Derain, Henri Matisse, Albert Marquet and Georges Rouault (*see* page 105), who successfully outraged contemporary art critics when they first exhibited their highly irregular and vibrantly coloured paintings in 1905 at the Paris Salon. As a style of painting, *Fauvism* (literally 'the wild beasts') both fed upon and influenced the other major contemporary movements of *Expressionism*, and *Cubism. See also Expressionism; Cubism.*

Fresco This is a form of wall-painting, normally in water-colour on plaster, and particularly suited to the climate of central Italy, where it has been practised since the early thirteenth century.

Genre painting This form of painting incorporates domestic scenes or incidents from everyday life.

Impressionism The most important artistic development of the nineteenth century, *Impressionism* grew out of the concern of mostly French artists, such as Monet, Renoir, Pissaro, Cézanne and Degas, to obtain a heightened sense of naturalism in their painting by exploring the sensual effects of light and colour on the surfaces of objects. *See also Neo-Impressionism; Post-Impressionism.*

Metaphysical Painting An Italian group of surrealist painters, founded during the First World War by Carlo Carra and Giorgio de Chirico (*see* page 94), this school set out to create a sense of wonder and mystery in an effort to capture the enigmatic quality of reality. This they did by experimenting with incongruous juxtapositions of naively treated classical forms.

Muralist This is the term used to describe an artist specialising in wall-paintings (murals), such as David Siqueiros (*see* page 106).

Nabi This name – derived from the Hebrew word for 'prophet' – was chosen by a group of French artists, among them Pierre Bonnard and Maurice Denis (*see* page 95), between 1889 and 1899. They were particularly inspired by Paul Gauguin's use of flat, pure colour as they swung away from the influence of *Impressionism. See also Symbolist Movement.*

Naive The term '*naive*' is generally used to describe any art characterized by a direct simplicity.

Neo-Impressionism Though also concerned with the effects of colour and light on objects, *Neo-Impressionism* has in fact little to do with *Impressionism*. Its principal exponent, Georges Seurat, contrived a technique, known as *Pointillism. See also Pointillism.*

Die Neue Sachlichkeit A phrase coined in 1923 to highlight a new attention to realistic, detailed representation in German painting, *Die Neue Sachlichkeit* (or 'New Objectivity') evolved as a reaction against *Expressionism* at the end of the First World War.

Pointillism This technique was employed by the *Neo-Impressionists* and involved painting entirely in small dots of pure colour, limited to those of the spectrum, and occasionally blended with white. When viewed from a distance, the dots merge to form brightly coloured objects. *See also Neo-Impressionism.*

Post-Impressionism This movement of artists, among them Vincent van Gogh, Paul Gauguin and Paul Cézanne, jettisoned the values of *Impressionism* and *Neo-Impressionism* in favour of a return to more formal composition and a greater emphasis on the subject of their works. *See also Impressionism; Neo-Impressionism.*

Sezession, Berlin One of a number of independent exhibiting societies formed during the 1890s by various groups of European artists, the *Berlin Sezession* played an important role in promoting the alternative art movements of its day.

Stijl, De An influential, avant-garde Dutch magazine (1917–28), initially concerned with successfully promoting the works of artists such as Piet Mondrian, *De Stijl* was later used as a platform for *Dada. See also Dada.*

Surrealism This form of art presents an attempt at representing and interpreting the phenomena of dreams or similar experiences.

Among its most important exponents are Giorgio de Chirico (*see* page 94), Salvador Dali (*see* page 95) and René Magritte (*see* page 100).

Symbolist Movement Those belonging to the *Symbolist Movement* used both objects and colour to suggest ideas or states of mind. Although a number of individuals are usually specifically identified with the *Symbolist Movement* – among them Gustav Moreau and Odilon Redon (*see* page 103) – its impact was very broad and can be seen in the work of artists as diverse as the *Nabi* and Gustav Klimt (*see* page 98). *See also Nabi.*

Synthetic Cubism This was a third phase of *Cubism*, often referred to as *Late Cubism*, and lasting approximately from 1912 to 1914. Practised chiefly by Juan Gris and Fernand Léger, as well as by Picasso and Braque, *Synthetic Cubism* evolved as the austerity of *Analytical Cubism* gave way to more lyrical, harmonious and colourful compositions. *See also Analytical Cubism; Cubism.*

Tempera Particularly important to medieval painters, *tempera* is any substance which 'tempers' powder colour and makes it workable. The most common and oldest form of *tempera* is egg yolk, which dries the paint almost instantly, several times lighter than normal, and in a hard permanent coat.

Triptych A picture, chiefly used as an altar-piece, and made in three parts.

Vorticists This was a school of English *Cubists*, founded in 1914 by Wyndham Lewis, who strove, through both painting and writing, to accelerate the establishment of a British equivalent to the European *avant-garde. See also Cubism.*

ADDITIONAL ACKNOWLEDGEMENTS

Nash – *Genesis*: courtesy The Paul Nash Trust; photos A.C. Cooper/Newman – *Be 1*: courtesy The Detroit Institute of Arts, Founders Society Purchase, W. Hawkins Ferry Fund and Mr and Mrs Walter B. Ford II Fund/Chagall – *Adam and Eve*: gift of Morton D May to The Saint Louis Art Museum/Szubert – *The Tower of Babel*: photo Ivy Studios/Ensor – *The Finding of Moses*: University of California, Berkeley. Gift of Joachim Jean Aberbach/Shahn – *Third Allegory*: photo Scala/Shalom of Safed – *Levites plaing music, in the Holy Temple*: photo Art Resource, New York/Klimt – *Judith II*: photo Scala/Rouault – *The Baptism of Christ*: photo Musées de la Ville de Paris/de Chirico – *The Prodigal Son*: photo Giraudon/Modersohn-Becker – *The Good Samaritan*: photo Lars Lohrisch/Beckmann – *Christ and the Woman taken in Adultery*: bequest of Curt Valentin/Schmidt-Rottluff – *The Pharisees*: Gertrud A. Mellon Fund/Dali – *The Sacrament of the Last Supper*: Chester Dale Collection, National Gallery of Art, Washington/Siqueiros – *Christ*: photo Scala/Picasso – *Crucifixion*: photo Scala/Gleizes – *Figure in Glory*: photo Martine Seyve-Cristofoli